The Intimacy Coordinator's Guidebook

The Intimacy Coordinator's Guidebook: Specialties for Stage and Screen explores the role of the intimacy choreographer with an in-depth look at specializations that exist within the profession.

With contributions by over 30 industry professionals, this book aims to bring awareness to a wide range of needs a project may have and how intimacy professionals use their cultural competency specialists in practice to create the most compelling storytelling. In Part One, the book addresses the scope of practice of an intimacy professional by discussing competency, finding your lens and tangential fields in the industry like fight directors, mental health coordinators and cultural competency specialists. Part Two covers specialties like working with minors, prosthetics, intimacy and disability, staging queer intimacy, working with fat actors, Black American intimacy, dance, working on scenes of trauma, sexual violence and non-consent, and BDSM. Between each chapter is a conversation with an actor, director or producer on their experiences working with an intimacy coordinator. In Part Three, the book looks at what it means to be qualified and intimacy professionals' hopes for the future of the industry.

The Intimacy Coordinator's Guidebook is an invaluable resource for directors and producers looking to hire an intimacy professional, as well as in-depth study for those who are training or practicing in the field of intimacy for performance.

Brooke M. Haney (they/she) is the creator of *The Actor's Warm Down*. They were one of the first 50 people in the world recognized by SAG/AFTRA on their registry of qualified intimacy coordinators. As an IC, Brooke has worked for CBS, HBO, Amazon Prime, Paramount+, Peacock, Disney, Warner Brothers and on numerous films. They are an actor with AEA and SAG/AFTRA and have their MFA in performance from the University of Central Florida.

The Intimacy Coordinator's Guidebook

Specialties for Stage and Screen

EDITED BY BROOKE M. HANEY

NEW YORK AND LONDON

Designed cover image: Master1305/Shutterstock.com

First published 2024
by Routledge
605 Third Avenue, New York, NY 10158

and by Routledge
4 Park Square, Milton Park, Abingdon, Oxon, OX14 4RN

Routledge is an imprint of the Taylor & Francis Group, an informa business

© 2024 selection and editorial matter, Brooke M. Haney; individual chapters, the contributors

The right of Brooke M. Haney to be identified as the author of the editorial material, and of the authors for their individual chapters, has been asserted in accordance with sections 77 and 78 of the Copyright, Designs and Patents Act 1988.

All rights reserved. No part of this book may be reprinted or reproduced or utilised in any form or by any electronic, mechanical, or other means, now known or hereafter invented, including photocopying and recording, or in any information storage or retrieval system, without permission in writing from the publishers.

Trademark notice: Product or corporate names may be trademarks or registered trademarks, and are used only for identification and explanation without intent to infringe.

ISBN: 978-1-032-53147-2 (hbk)
ISBN: 978-1-032-53146-5 (pbk)
ISBN: 978-1-003-41055-3 (ebk)

DOI: 10.4324/9781003410553

To Tarana Burke, founder of the "me too" movement.

And to those who gave it visibility in the entertainment industry.

You created awareness around the abuse in the industry and built momentum for change that ultimately birthed this profession that I love.

I firmly believe that we don't always know when we bless someone.

Each of you has blessed me with your courage and advocacy.

I hope this book will continue to bless those who read it, who will go on to bless the folk they support on set and on stage.

Contents

Foreword by Chelsea Pace   *xi*
Acknowledgments   *xiv*

Introduction   1
by Brooke M. Haney

INTRODUCTION TO PART ONE
Scope of Practice   **5**
by Brooke M. Haney

1. Competency   8
   Brooke M. Haney

2. Finding Your Lens   15
   Brooke M. Haney

3. Cultural Competency Specialist   20
   Chels Morgan

4. Intimacy and Violence   25
   Moderated by Cha Ramos

5. Mental Health Coordination   31
   Amanda Edwards, with contribution from Bridget McCarthy

INTRODUCTION TO PART TWO
Specialities   **37**
by Brooke M. Haney

6   International Considerations   40
    Cessalee Stovall

    A Conversation with Nesta Cooper   47

7   Working with Minors   52
    Kim Shively

    A Conversation with Grace Byers   57

8   Intimacy and Disability   62
    Brooke M. Haney

    A Conversation with Ryan J. Haddad   69

9   Working with Fat Actors   74
    Katherine Blouse and Brooke M. Haney

    A Conversation with Jen Ponton   80

10   Black American Intimacy: Considerations for Choreography and Practice   85
    Kaja Dunn

    A Conversation with Tai Leshaun   95

11   Queer Intimacy   100
    Raja Benz, Leo Mock, Robbie Taylor Hunt, and Brooke M. Haney

    A Conversation with Becca Blackwell   118

| 12 | BDSM
Olivia "Troy" Troy | 122 |

A Conversation with Midori   128

| 13 | Rope Scenes
Megan Gilron and Brooke M. Haney | 132 |

A Conversation with Michael Emery   138

| 14 | Stories of Trauma
Brooke M. Haney | 142 |

A Conversation with Amnon Lourie and Nate Dushku   149

| 15 | Non-Consent and Sexual Violence
Amy Northup | 155 |

A Conversation with Olivia Luccardi   164

| 16 | Intimacy and Dance
Brooke M. Haney with contributions from Sara Lozoff and Nicole Perry | 168 |

A Conversation with Jimmy Smits   174

| 17 | Prosthetics
Amanda Liz Cutting, with additional credits to Anastasia St. Amand, Dave Trainor, Amelia Smart, Principal Intimacy Professionals, and The National Society of Intimacy Professionals | 179 |

INTRODUCTION TO PART THREE
Moving Forward   **187**
Brooke M. Haney

| 18 | The Intimacy Captain
Brooke M. Haney with contributions from Ann James | 189 |

19 Qualification *Brooke M. Haney*	192
20 Adapting to the Actor's Process *Laura Rikard*	198
21 Hopes for the Industry *Moderated by Brooke M. Haney*	203
Index	*213*

Foreword
By Chelsea Pace

In 2022, I had come home from rehearsal and I was sitting in Brooke's living room with their now-fiancé, Katie. Over a board game, Brooke made the case for collecting a diverse group of perspectives on the work and on best practices in intimacy coordination. Capturing perspectives from not just the highly visible, majority-white figures in the field, but from the specialists, thought leaders and stakeholders that maybe even conflicted with or complicated those perspectives. It was a brilliant idea, and I think the service that this book provides is a very valuable one in collecting so many of those voices.

Diversity of practice and thought is a gift, not a liability. If you are in a conversation with an opponent of consent-based practice, it might be valuable to flatten those perspectives and present a united front to help justify the existence of an intimacy professional on set. But our field should not be built as a weapon to defeat the resistance of our detractors. The field of intimacy coordination should be built in a way that only a field of people who think deeply about power, ethics, communication and storytelling could.

White supremacy and capitalism herd all of us towards flattening complex ideas and multiple perspectives into one easy-to-digest nugget. I understand the allure of a single vision, but it is not the reality, nor is it for the best. Maybe one day we will get to a place where every intimacy coordinator has deeply reflected on all that they know and have learned about the work and the world and they will reach the same conclusions. We aren't there yet, and this fledgling period of our field's development is a special, tenuous one. I don't think we should rush it.

The work of figuring out a way to stage an intimate scene is old – even though the procedures and titles are new. There haven't always been qualified, thoughtful people there to help facilitate that process, but now there can be, if we help each other get into those rooms. The goal of the field at this moment can be to get more thoughtful intimacy people onto more sets.

The film industry will keep making film and television with or without us – I think it is in our best interest as a field to spend our energy holding the door open.

In the early days of the field, the few establishing intimacy professionals were under a lot of pressure to not only know everything (and defend it fiercely), but to be everything to everyone. Now an emerging intimacy coordinator can gain critical experience on a project that aligns with their skill level. No longer going it alone, they can (and should) build a support network of fellow coordinators to develop alongside as they create their own iteration of an intimacy practice. Rather than being everything to everyone, they can choose to specialize in serial storytelling, short films, non-consensual stories, stories that talk about intimacies beyond the physical – intimacies of identity. The diversification of practice and specialty is not only necessary but an incredible opportunity for every intimacy coordinator: if we work to make room in the field, there will be someone with the right specialty and practice for every project, leaving us each space to give our time and expertise to the stories that most excite us.

About fifteen years ago I started doing the work that I would now call intimacy work. I found bits and pieces of consent-based storytelling, boundary establishment practices and choreographic techniques. I made stuff up and tried it out. Over many years and with the help of many collaborators, I pulled together little scraps and threads that were woven together and modified and brought into whatever the most current understanding of consent and boundaries and artistic ethics was. My book, *Staging Sex: Best Practices, Tools, and Techniques*, was the first book on the subject of staging intimacy, but, thankfully, it is already no longer the only book on the subject. I think the work in this book compliments *Staging Sex* beautifully. I wrote a general overview with broadly applicable techniques, but *The Intimacy Coordinator's Guidebook: Specialties for Stage and Screen* shows us some of the many paths on which those techniques can be applied.

In a discipline where we are often a department of one, it is a precious opportunity to learn about the specializations and practices of our colleagues. How lucky are we to have them gathered here? This burgeoning field has come such a long way since I wrote the first outline for the book that would become *Staging Sex*. The field has come even further since I started asking questions about consent, storytelling and the way we told stories of intimacy. I certainly wasn't alone in those early days, but, in many ways, all of the people searching for the early foundations of this work were finding their way in the dark.

Not anymore. The sun is shining on this field of ours and we are all so fortunate to be in the company of these brilliant thinkers and artists. The specialties on these pages capture where we are as the intimacy coordinators, class of 2023. I look forward to seeing the places where my practice will grow and change and I hope that the field will grow outward and upward from this point. How lucky are we to be in this work together?

Acknowledgments

People say that writing can be a lonely job. However, so many people supported me in this process that it didn't feel lonely at all.

Thank you to:

All the directors, producers, actors and crew that I have worked with and learned from over my lifetime so far. This book would not be possible without those experiences.

Everyone who asked me about the book, encouraged me or celebrated the ideas behind it. Your encouragement was awesome, and your curiosity allowed me to verbally process my ideas and hone in on what I wanted to say.

Everyone who wrote for this book, allowed me to interview them for this book and the PR teams who helped set up those interviews. I could not have accomplished my goal of a diversity of thought without each of you.

Chelsea Pace for supporting me as a friend and colleague, being there the night I first pitched the idea, encouraging me, responding to texts, taking long phone calls to process a hurdle or difficult concept, and for introducing me to Stacey Walker, my wonderful editor at Routledge.

Stacey for believing in me and in this book.

Lucia Accorsi who became my guide at Routledge along the way.

Felichia Chivaughn Ellison for reading the book and giving me incredible notes based on her own experience and expertise in this field.

Faith Marsland for her efficiency and incredible attention to detail as copy editor.

Kris Šiošytė, Senior Production Editor at Taylor & Francis Books, for guiding me through the production process with clarity and ease.

Acknowledgments xv

My agent Sara Alexander, as well as Reuben Stauber and Brooke Bretschger at Alexander Creatives. I'm so lucky to be represented by you and grateful for the support.

The teachers who influenced me and championed my career starting in elementary school and all the way through graduate study: Michelle Omli Wentroble, who gave me my first paid choreography job when I was in seventh grade; Allyn Turner, my high school drama teacher; Eeva Reeder, my high school math teacher, biggest champion and friend; Susie Miller, my volleyball coach who taught me the value of being pushed and taking a note; and my professors: Susan Appel, Tracy Bersley, Geraldine Clark, Elizabeth Ingram, Chris Fisher, Robyn Hunt, Mark Brotherton, Jim Helsinger, Kate Ingram, Julia Listengarten and Earl Weaver.

The incredible practitioners in the intimacy industry who didn't write for the book, but supported it in other valuable ways: Ash Anderson, Karyn Mott, Phay Moores, Judi Lewis Ockler, Heather Ondersma, Britta Joy Peterson, Alicia Rodis and Claire Warden.

Valerie Clayman Pye and Amanda Rose Villarreal who supported Laura Rikard.

Annie Paul, my bessie, for your feedback and late night phone calls to process. You know me and my writing about as well as anyone and your thoughtful insight was incredibly valuable.

Ellen Adair, my accountability partner and friend, who weekly listened to my goals and progress, encouraged me and gave advice when asked.

Alex Alberto, Kendall Bossert, Julie Fry, Molly Powers Gallagher, Nikki Gepner, Alexis McGuiness, Danna Shaner, Daniel Morgan Shelley, Kristen Tomanocy and Grace Trimble for being friends I could bounce ideas off of, vent to, and celebrate with.

My family, especially: Jaime Cumming, Hal Reeder, Terry Reeder, Kirsten Myres, Rose Myres.

Jeff and Sue Blouse for being a constant encouragement and cheerleaders of my career.

The folks at Red Pipes Cafe in Forest Hills where I wrote about a quarter of the book.

The treadmills at Planet Fitness in Forest Hills which graciously served as walking desks.

Katie Blouse, my partner (soon to be wife) and my love, who not only wrote a chapter in the book with me, but supported me by reading chapters, giving feedback and bringing me dinner when I was on a roll. Your support was and continues to be life and passion affirming.

Lastly, thank you to Liz Mattera. Liz is an incredible actor who, while supporting me on this book, was also thriving in her own artistic career. I write about disability in this book and sometimes having a disability means that situations that could be joyful are dimmed because of the challenges they present. Liz did all of the work on this book that doesn't come naturally for me. When something needed to be done that might have made me feel overwhelmed or easily frustrated, I sent an email or text to Liz and she took care of it. Her support removed the distractions from my process and, as a result, I was able to focus on places where I am passionate. Because of Liz, I wrote this book with ease and felt only joy. Thank you, thank you, thank you!

Introduction

Brooke M. Haney

I curated this book because I wanted to read it. I was hungry for a book that brought a bunch of voices from the intimacy community together in conversation about where we believed we should be competent and what specialties exist. Afterall, no one would expect every stunt coordinator to be proficient at every skill. There are excellent riggers, folks that specialize in scenes in the water, or those who work a lot with fire. It seemed to me that a book addressing scope of practice in the field of intimacy, as well as competencies and specialties, was needed.

When Routledge did commission me to write it, I was beyond excited to ask the amazing people in this book to collaborate with me. This industry, while still in its early years, is full of incredible practitioners. I believe a diversity of thought is necessary to building the best foundation, so it was with incredible joy and deep responsibility that I selected the folks who wrote these chapters.

It felt important that there wasn't an overwhelm of folks from one organization or philosophy, so I have endeavored to bring together a group that is composed of independent intimacy choreographers as well as some that are running training companies. I have so many incredible colleagues that I couldn't have possibly invited everyone I would have liked to write for this book. Routledge was able to offer a small stipend for 11 of the contributors in this book. This was, for me, a deal breaker when negotiating this contract, as folks should be paid for their work and expertise. Often, especially in the theatre, folks are asked to contribute their labor for free in exchange for exposure. Exposure is incredibly important in a new industry, especially if you are a thought leader and want to make sure you are being credited for your ideas, and folks should

DOI: 10.4324/9781003410553-1

still be paid for that work. However, it should be noted that Megan Gilron, Ann James, Sarah Lozoff, Amy Northup, Laura Rikard, NIcole Perry and Chelsea Pace volunteered their contributions so that other folks could be paid more. All the voices I have found are special and I am incredibly grateful to each of them for contributing their time, talent and voice to this book.

And here's the thing about a diversity of thought: we won't all agree. I don't align with everything other folks have written. Certainly there are things I've written that others may take issue with and there are ideas that may conflict. This is good. There isn't only one, correct way to do this work. When I asked folks to write, I didn't look for the person I knew was right, I selected folks who were breaking ground and whose work I admire and asked them to write about their process.

This book can only be an introduction to these ideas. Each chapter could be its own book. My hope is that, as you read it, you will get a greater sense of what goes into working on specialized material and know better how to supplement your learning.

Who this book is written for

For **working intimacy professionals** as well as **those in training**, this book will serve as a conversation with your colleagues. I hope that it deepens your thought about your own practice and encourages you to become even more clear about where your specialties and competencies lie and where you might desire a consultant or seek out more training. The clearer we can be about our scope of practice, the more consent-forward the spaces we create will be, and our storytelling will be more compelling.

For **producers and directors**, this book is aimed at helping you to better understand what is within the scope of an intimacy professional. Additionally, it is here to help you clarify the kinds of needs that your project might have and give you the language to better interview intimacy professionals so that you can hire the best possible teammate to support you.

There is a scarcity mentality in our industry, especially for **actors**, and when a job is on offer it can be more difficult to tune into your needs. Your desire to please and keep the job or get the next job might be intense. While an intimacy professional creates space for boundaries to be expressed, we can't know what yours are unless you can articulate them. Use this opportunity, while the stakes are low, to consider your needs and boundaries. The best thing you can do is teach your body that it can trust you. Consider discovering your boundaries and being disciplined about articulating them as an essential part of your training. I hope this book also builds excitement for the expansive opportunities to tell stories with your body. As you read, I encourage you to ask yourself: what kinds of work do you want to do? What can you do to train your body to be ready to execute the demands of the choreography? What needs do you have or what questions might you want to ask an intimacy professional when you are in conversation with one about a role or a scene in order to be able to do your best work?

For **other folks who interact with intimacy professionals (crew, stage managers, designers, etc.**): I hope that reading this book gives you a greater sense of what kinds of work you may be asked to support and what that may look like, encouragement to work on your own to clarify your boundaries, and information about how to include an intimacy professional in your process.

Regarding vocabulary

An **intimacy professional** (**IP**) in film and TV is usually called an **intimacy coordinator** (**IC**), while in theatre they are often called an **intimacy director** (**ID**). Intimacy consultant, designer and choreographer are also terms that are commonly used. In this book, individual writers will write from the perspective of the media where they most commonly work. As a note, I've noticed some folks in the entertainment industry and academia referring to this job as an "intimacy coach." This is incorrect. An intimacy coach is someone who coaches individuals, couples or multiple partners on their actual sex life. Everything intimacy choreographers create is simulated. While as a rule I believe that folks should call themselves the title that feels most right to them, I do encourage you to avoid intimacy coach.

Some notes on how to read the book

This book is divided into three parts. The first will cover scope of practice and finding your lens. Part Two will contain chapters written by different intimacy professionals, discussing specialties at which they are leaders in the field. Between the chapters in Part Two, I have included interviews with actors, directors, writers and producers who have worked with intimacy coordinators to give anecdotes and advice. Finally, part three will discuss how to know someone is qualified, how intimacy coordinators can adapt their process to the needs of individual actors and a final-look interview with a group of intimacy professionals on their hopes for the industry.

If a chapter is written by someone other than me, it will say so. If it doesn't have someone else credited, I wrote it. Occasionally, there will be a chapter where I interviewed someone and wrote about their ideas. When this is the case, I will make that clear at the top of the chapter.

This book is an introduction to some advanced concepts. As such, if someone uses a word you don't know, look it up. I had to do that several times reading the chapters by my colleagues.

While I hope that you will read the whole book, if your project contains content that is addressed in Part Two, feel free to jump ahead and read that chapter. Those chapters are meant to stand alone within the larger framework of the book. However, consider reading Part One in conversation with that chapter for broader context on scope of practice.

Content note

This book will include discussion of many types of intimacy, consensual and non-consensual, including: sexual assault, racism, sexism, homophobia, BDSM, kink, adult language, etc. When chapters choose to describe something in detail, there will be a separate note at the beginning of the chapter. However, if a chapter is merely going to mention something without describing it, there won't be a specific content note.

Introduction to Part One
Scope of Practice
Brooke M. Haney

Before jumping into specialties, let's set a foundation for ourselves. Though there are many ways to train and become qualified, there is an assumption that working intimacy choreographers all have a basic set of knowledge and skills. Part One will dive into those competencies as well as define the difference between a competency and a specialty. Then, we'll talk about how to find your lens and your area of expertise. Finally, we'll address an intimacy professional's scope of practice by looking at several fields that are closely aligned with intimacy coordinators – cultural competency specialists, fight directors and mental health coordinators.

By the end of Part One, you should have a clear vocabulary around what is and isn't the job of a qualified intimacy professional, and be ready to start looking at specialties in the industry.

From Kim Shively

To understand scope of practice or the concept of one's "lane," I look to the role of the *doula*. Understanding this position can be informative when thinking about the responsibilities of the IC. A doula is the formalized support position for a laboring person. The doula supports the process of childbirth by providing information so that the laboring person and their family can make informed decisions, often standing to the side, observing and ready, but only getting involved when and as needed. To be a qualified doula, the person undergoes training to help understand the process of pregnancy, birth, hospital culture and procedure, and the post-partum period (www.dona.org). Because doulas often work in hospitals, it is essential that the doula understands their unique *scope of practice* as well as the roles of everyone else in the hospital.

The role of the intimacy coordinator (IC) involves a similar process. The IC needs to understand not only the actor process, but the culture and hierarchy of a set and the process of pre- and post-production. The role requires competency in choreographic language and training in additional tools like barrier garments and props. Like the doula, the IC serves as a mediator and should have excellent communication skills and the ability to read situations and respond proactively. And, ultimately, the IC will often stand to the side, observing and ready, but only becoming involved when and as needed.

Things to Consider

For Intimacy Professionals

- Do I have these competencies or are there areas I still want to learn about or work on?
- Do I have a clear sense of my scope of practice?
- Can I clearly articulate my process?
- How would I describe my lens to a director or producer in an interview?

For Directors and Producers

- Do I have a clear understanding of the role of an intimacy professional and how that is different from a stunt coordinator or fight director, mental health coordinator or cultural coordinator?
- Do I have a sense of when I need to budget for any of these roles?

For Actors

- Do I understand the difference between an intimacy professional, stunt coordinator or fight director, and cultural competency specialist?
- Which of these positions have I worked with on set or in rehearsal so far?
- When working with an intimacy professional, what was most helpful or what seems like it would be helpful?
- Do I feel prepared to advocate for one of these roles if a project I'm cast in would benefit from one?

Competency 1

Brooke M. Haney

There is a certain level of training and competency that every intimacy professional should have. As you begin to read Part Two of the book and encounter the specialties, you might first think, by having some competency in an area, that means you already specialize in it. For example, I have significant experience in the BDSM/kink community and have done a lot of research into that world. However, in talking with Troy and reading her chapter in Part Two, I realized that I had a high level of competency in some areas, but wasn't yet a specialist. As that is an area of great importance to me, I doubled down on my research, focusing on the areas I still needed. I hope that some of you will have this same, joyful opportunity for increased learning.

> Beyond the basics of boundaries, consent, choreography and closure, most intimacy professionals, regardless of their identity or experience, should have a level of competency in many other areas. Going beyond competency into deep research and understanding is what makes someone a specialist.

Before we jump into specialties, let's all get on the same page about what competencies are expected of intimacy professionals. While different training programs offer classes in many of these things, or recommend ways to find this learning, it is up to you to look inward and assess if that learning has truly made you competent in the area and ready to be an intimacy practitioner. Practicing before you are ready may unintentionally cause harm, and, especially while the industry is still new, it is of high importance that we operate above reproach. That isn't to say that we won't make mistakes – we will. However, practicing on real people, before you are ready, will have consequences not just in that micro situation, but in the macro.

Cultural Competency

Later in Part One, Chels Morgan will write on the position of cultural competency specialist. Working with a cultural competency specialist is an excellent idea, and doesn't relieve you of the responsibility for being culturally competent. This means more than taking a DEI class or a basic gender and sexuality class on how to use pronouns. If you feel anxious about how to talk with folks of a different race, gender expression or sexuality, that likely means that you care **and** that you have more learning to do. It's okay to not be perfect; perfection isn't real. However, media is a powerful tool and, without doing deep work in this area, you risk reinforcing harmful tropes as well as being ignorant of or ill equipped to navigate moments of harm in production. You do not need to be an expert, ready to dramaturg a specific story, but you do need to know how both history and current events affect the dynamics on set that your actors are experiencing as well as how the choreography you are creating will be experienced by an audience.

Non-Apparent Disability

According to *Forbes Magazine*, "over 42 million Americans have a severe disability, and 96% of them are unseen." Considering this, it is unethical to work as an intimacy professional without a certain level of competency with non-apparent disabilities, how to support them and how to discuss them with actors and production. If the program you train with doesn't offer courses on working with folks with non-apparent disability, you are ethically obligated to supplement your training elsewhere. While mental illnesses are disabilities, merely getting mental health certification is not enough. Ideally, we would all have competency around working with folks with apparent disabilities as well. However, I recognize that with the incredibly limited representation of apparent disabilities and how exclusionary the industry is of actors with apparent disabilities, this type of work is currently more of a specialty, which is why it is covered in Part Two.

Size Competency

Historically, our industry has perpetuated an incredibly narrow idea of the size of the human body. Actors were almost exclusively small, white people with occasionally taller men and larger character roles in which intimacy almost never existed, unless as a joke. As the industry begins to expand a bit, we must be prepared. To that end, we need to be competent in working with fat actors, both around liberating language and choreography. While this should be a competency that all IPs have, due to the lack of representation of intimacy with fat characters, I've included a chapter in Part Two on working with fat actors as well.

Mental Health First Aid

It can be difficult to find a mental health first aid class that applies that learning specifically to our field. To my mind, taking mental health first aid is like taking medical first aid and CPR – all adult humans should do it. It is a basic foundation for moving about the world. It's not that it makes you instantly a better IP, it's simply that if you don't have it, you probably shouldn't be doing this work.

Power Dynamics

The foundation of our work is bringing awareness to power dynamics, broadly in the entertainment industry, and specifically in the project we are working on. It is nuanced and no two projects are going to be exactly the same, so it should be the first thing you think about in your risk assessment. Some things to take into account: race and other identities, class, prestige or celebrity, amount of time in the industry, relationships and position (for example, is a producer or a director also an actor in the scene?). All these things affect the power dynamics in the room.

Bystander Intervention

Bystander intervention is of utmost importance for intimacy professionals. Witnessing someone harm someone else will understandably put many people into fight, flight, freeze or fawn. When we are working as an intimacy professional, this can't happen to us. It is our job to be the bystander who acts. I personally love Right To Be's bystander intervention training, and have taken many of their free online classes. I appreciate the way that they include history or cultural context for each of their training sessions. Additionally, the 5Ds – distract, delegate, document, delay and direct – give specific actionable strategies for handling a situation when it does arise. As intimacy professionals, we can both plan which of the 5Ds we feel most equipped to use in the moment, and we always document everything in our reports as well.

Trauma Informed Practices

Let's face it, as a result of Covid-19, everyone has experienced some level of trauma. While we can't create a completely safe space, working with trauma informed practices is a necessity. Many of our best practices naturally have a trauma informed approach, such as building trust through transparency around expectations, empowering actors to assert their boundaries, offering choices, incorporating a historically and culturally competent approach to our work, and creating a saf**er** space for brave collaboration.

Risk Assessment

Among the first things an intimacy coordinator will do when looking at a project is a risk assessment. This starts with breaking down a script to see when and where we might be needed as well as challenges that may arise due to the content, budget, locations, time and power dynamics. As you read through the chapters on specialties, consider what additional needs and risks may arise due to the nature of and specifics of the project.

Boundaries and Consent

Perhaps the most basic part of our job is making space for the actors to express their boundaries and consent for the actions a project requires of them. Being truly competent in this area means being able to make space without being precious. An inexperienced or hypervigilant IC can make the whole team feel like they are walking on eggshells. Boundaries and consent are a foundational element of our work, and should be shared and honored with ease.

Masking

Whether you are masking a kiss, a body part or a moment of simulated sex, the tools to do this are a necessary part of this job. Having a variety of options in mind, such as positioning or using props or set pieces, will help give the director a feeling of expansiveness in the storytelling while allowing the actor to feel ease in their boundaries.

Modesty Garments and Barriers

An intimacy coordinator will have a kit that they rent out daily or weekly that will include a lot of what they need on set. However, there are also items that will need to be purchased for projects. Modesty garments should be purchased both in the actor's skin tone and sized to fit them. Most modesty garment companies carry a range of skin tones and either have garments that can be cut to fit or will custom make a size for you at no additional charge, but you must plan time for this process. I like to include the actors in this ordering process when possible so that they can have a say in their garment and have the confidence in advance that they will have the correct garment on set. I coordinate with wardrobe and will send the actor a link to some options online, and ask them to select what is best for them. This is also good rule of thumb for prosthetics if they aren't being custom made.

Choreography

This is the fun part! (At least to me.) There are many different movement vocabularies that work for choreographing intimacy. Some folks got into this industry through the fight or stunt world, some through dance or Laban, some through acting, etc. Whether you have a movement background or have pursued this skill as part of your intimacy training, it is one of the most important ones, because this is where we express our artistry.

Due to the pandemic, a lot of intimacy training went online. As a result, the industry wasn't stagnant and we have a wealth of new intimacy professionals. However, this also meant that there wasn't a lot of hands-on training in choreography. Even those with previous choreographic skills might understandably feel rusty. If you feel like you need to learn or brush up on how to choreograph, there are options: watch scenes of intimacy and notate them, take dance or stage combat choreography classes, read up on choreographic vocabulary and create movement plots to practice.

Closure

Closure practices are tools for actors to let go of their characters or the given circumstances of the story. The closure tools we have can be very effective for actors to use in addition to their own self-care. Those tools should not be confused with mental health care. Closure is an important skill for actors to work on themselves, and an intimacy choreographer can offer tools, help facilitate learning, and make space and time for it in a production. Having a variety of options for solo to partnered activities as well as ones that require a range as far as time commitment is ideal.

Coordination and Management

Attention to detail and project management skills are necessary when coordinating with other departments. While the intimacy profession started as a department of one with occasionally a shadow or assistant, that most often isn't sufficient. We cannot demonstrate choreography on actors and lots of folks are visual learners. So, much like fight directors and stunt coordinators work in teams, intimacy departments are doing that as well. On set, it is beneficial for one IC to work with the first team and another with the second team. Or, if there are a large number of actors involved in the scene, whether it be principal or background talent, having more than one person on set to check with talent between takes can make sets run more efficiently. To that end, if you are the head of your intimacy team, having management skills and a style is important for workplace culture and effectiveness.

Adapting Our Practice

Being rooted in a pedagogy is good, and being rigid doesn't serve. We learn and set up best practices for our work, and, in the moment, we must be flexible to adapt to the needs of the director, actors, project and situation.

Scope of Practice

These competencies are all things within the scope of practice of an intimacy professional. As you read further in Part One, we will address parallel positions that are complementary to IPs, but whose scope of practice is different and not to be confused with our job.

Bibliography

Morgan, Paula. (2022) "Invisible Disabilities: Break down the Barriers." *Forbes Magazine*, October 12, https://www.forbes.com/sites/paulamorgan/2020/03/20/invisible-disabilities-break-down-the-barriers/?sh=5636d19efa50.

Finding Your Lens   2

Brooke M. Haney

You've completed your training. Hooray! You are feeling competent and qualified to start taking jobs. Awesome. As you start to think about your own work as an intimacy choreographer, consider and be intentional about the lens through which you create. Our lens is heavily influenced by how we were brought up, who we surround ourselves with, our experiences and what media we've ingested.

> Identity doesn't equal experience, and experience doesn't equal expertise.

Identity

When I talk with young folks who are questioning their sexuality, I often say to them that you can be queer without having to prove it. I'm bisexual (or pansexual). I fall in love with a person, not a gender. And that would be true if I'd never slept with a woman or a man or a genderfluid person or anyone at all. Being currently partnered with a woman doesn't make me a lesbian, though I don't mind that term and sometimes use it. My identity is my identity regardless of my experience.

It is reasonable and important to honor when folks want artistic collaborators who have the experience of the characters and story. Not having to code switch or explain things to folks outside of that identity can be really useful. It can also go a long way toward authentic storytelling, because there is less of an opportunity for someone outside of the community's lens to be put on the story. That said, identity doesn't equal expertise.

When we get caught up thinking that identity equals expertise, the industry loses. For example, there are some BIPOC intimacy professionals that specialize in choreographing intimacy and race or racially charged work. However, that doesn't mean that every BIPOC intimacy choreographer specializes in that type of content. Furthermore, it is imperative that we don't hire BIPOC folks for only BIPOC stories. That would be robbing the world of a whole host of possibilities. Many BIPOC folks, especially Black women, have been doing the work of the intimacy industry around boundaries and consent for decades. By limiting their scope, we miss out on having some of the most experienced and most qualified people on set. Similarly, having queer and Trans choreographers on sets that are telling heterosexual stories of intimacy will greatly expand the scope of intimacy we see on stage and screen. Because the queer community has such a vast definition of sex, we tend to look at a larger picture and finer details.

Experience

There is really no substitute for personal experience and it is certainly a first step toward expertise. However, someone can be steeped in a culture or experience and not be intentionally observing it and translating it into storytelling. In order for experience to be turned into expertise, it must be analyzed and supplemented with observation and research.

Expertise

Choosing what you want to be an expert at is super fun. You have this great foundation of competency as an intimacy professional and now you get to decide where you want to focus. Of course it's totally awesome if you simply want to be a generalist. When you get the itch, though, finding a particular niche is exhilarating. Being an expert in a particular specialty means that you understand the history, culture, motivations and variety of a particular type of sex. There are many ways in which we can find that expertise, and the first place to start is with the interest and desire to learn. Of course, there are some specialties, like working on scenes involving water, that don't necessarily need a deep dive on history, unless the rest of the story indicates it, but many of the specialties in this book do benefit from that kind of study.

Media's Influence

The tricky thing about finding your own lens is that the media has a heavy influence over us. This can be a fantastic thing if there is a particular style you like and want to emulate. I really enjoy Ita O'Brien's work on *Normal People* and *I Will Destroy You*. Knowing that, I can look up her IMDB to see what other work I might want to watch in order to study her choreography. The same can be said for a director or actor one admires.

On the flip side, the media has been run (produced, directed, financed, created) for most of its existence by white, cisgendered, straight men. This narrow lens has been put on a lot of the stories we have seen. Just studying and replicating the stories of intimacy we've seen over the years will perpetuate inaccurate and less imaginative storytelling. This lens has mostly assumed that all people have sex like white people and all people have sex like straight people. In fact, I've heard white intimacy professionals say, "I'm not an expert in race, but I can choreograph sex." Those two things could be true, and it is dangerous to assume that identity doesn't impact the ways in which folks express intimacy.

Developing (or Changing) Your Lens

Begin by evaluating where you're starting from; what's your baseline? For example, when I wanted to specialize in queer stories, I had to acknowledge that I was raised straight and cis and that I was in monogamous, hetero facing relationships for the first three decades of my life. Additionally, I was raised very religious and we didn't go to movies or have a TV, so my exposure to queerness was incredibly limited. Even though I was queer, my lens was not. Certainly if I'd had more queer representation in my life growing up, I would have come out earlier and my lens would be different. When I did realize I was bisexual and genderqueer, I knew I needed an education on sex and my community. So, every day for a year, I took a class, or watched something, or listened to a podcast, or read something all about queer (and kinky) sex and took the time to evaluate how what I was learning could translate into storytelling. That year was hugely beneficial, and, as this is one of my specialties, I continue to study and research.

Every person's journey will be different. By acknowledging where you're starting, you can find a way to either develop your current lens or work to change your lens to the one you want it to be.

Whose Voice Is Centered

In talking with Kaja Dunn about our work in specialties, she reminded me:

> [W]hiteness will find a way to center itself and is drawn to any marginalization that can center whiteness. So when you start to talk about race, inevitably, a participant will mention disabilities, class, or sexual orientation. These are serious marginalization issues but I point out that you can center a body of color in any of these identities. It is not either or. It is intersectional and you cannot subtract racial hierarchies from the conversation.

Considering this, if you are a white person looking to specialize in an area, it is imperative that you have a strong competency in how race intersects with your specialty, and not only in specialties that might be considered marginalizations. For example, in the BDSM and kink communities, much of the language, dynamics, props and toys are rooted in racial oppression. As Catherine Scott says:

> [B]lack feminists have long defended black women's right to be counted as both sexy and sexual, without being accused of racial disloyalty. But when we add domination, whips, and chains to the mix, things get more complicated. Hardly surprising, given that much of the language surrounding BDSM involves those loaded words "master" and "slave."

Morgan Oddie adds: "By deliberately or unintentionally ignoring race, there is considerable risk of the perpetuation of tacitly racist, neoliberal and hegemonic ideologies about sexuality and intimacy." As intimacy professionals, our role is meant to disrupt power structures and be an advocate to the less powerful. If we instead take part in reinforcing power structures and societal ideas in our storytelling, either willingly or through ignorance, we are failing at our job. We get to be aware of these intersections and intentional about our work.

Scope of Practice

It is possible to confuse another job as a specialty within the intimacy industry. There are several positions that are parallel to an IP, and it is important to identify them as separate positions. The next three chapters are about three roles that can sometimes be confused as part of the scope of practice of an intimacy professional. Some of us are multi-hyphenates and do work in multiple positions. When that is the case, it is important for production to realize that they are hiring one person to fulfill two roles, and pay accordingly. Additionally, it is important for us to be clear with our cast and artistic team which of our responsibilities fall under which title, so that we aren't creating a misunderstanding around the role of an intimacy professional.

Bibliography

Oddie, Morgan. "'Playing' With Race: BDSM, Race Play, and Whiteness in Kink." *Panic at the Discourse*, www.panicdiscourse.com/playing-with-race/.

Scott, Catherine. (2012) "Thinking Kink: Playing with Race in BDSM." *Bitch Media*, August 6, www.bitchmedia.org/post/thinking-kink-bdsm-and-playing-with-race-sex-sexuality.

Cultural Competency Specialist

3

Chels Morgan, CSE

> Mx. Chels Morgan is an Afro-Latinx, queer and neuroexpansive sexuality and justice educator, intimacy coordinator, intimacy director, and cultural sensitivity specialist. They have developed curriculum on disability justice and accessibility, racial justice and intersectionality, trauma responsiveness and transformative justice, BDSM and kink, non-monogamy and polyamory, and queer theory and identity. There were so many things I would have loved to have them write about and I am thrilled they chose to write about their experience in cultural competency.

Cultural Competency – *in performance* – *(v.)* A verb. As in, active, actionable steps toward building accountable, justice-centered and anti-racist performance processes, centering impact over intent in our storytelling, and curating an industry that actively opposes ableism, cissexism, erotophobia, anti-blackness and all other systems used by white supremacy culture to oppress us.

"Cultural Competency," Mx. Chels Morgan, mxcmorgan.com

Who are you outside of yourself? Outside of the identities that walk with you – where your race, gender, sexuality, spirituality and all other unique classifications of human-ness, both discovered and unknown, find themselves divinely blending in perfect balance – outside of your identity and experience, who are you? For some of us, the answer to that is simple. We are friends, parents, children and siblings. We are mentors, leaders, artists and athletes. We are more than our races, more than our sexualities and more than our genders. However, for others, that question is much less simple. For some of us, to separate our individual labels from those we hold in our community is to see us for less than what we are. To speak for myself, using my own identities as the example, to see me outside of my Blackness, my Latinidad, my queerness and my neurodivergence is to see me incompletely and, in certain moments, it's to not see me at all.

For me and for many others like me, the space between being identified as a person vs. specifically a Black person or a queer person or an autistic person, is the space between encouraging my growth and facilitating my trauma. It's the space between standing strong in my perspective and making myself small to appease those in power, choosing dissociation over defiance.

And, perhaps most importantly for those in the intimacy coordination and direction community, it's the space between leading our actors to informed consent and leading them toward forced compliance, and that is where the potential for harm lives.

Intimacy as Precedent

There's good news. We've seen this before. With the introduction of intimacy directors into theatrical processes, we have found an influx of methodologies and praxes for how to integrate consent-based practices into performance spaces. Actors are able to sink deeper into their art and are making bolder choices. Directors don't have to fear pushing their actors to cross lines or encroaching upon their casts' limits. Intimacy on stage and screen has made a noticeable shift from actors improv-ing just to hit story beats to artists collaborating in order to tell truly beautiful, intimate stories.

However, while inclusive language and intimacy calls have helped to mitigate some of the harms this industry has perpetuated, multiple marginalized communities have still found themselves placed in positions that infringe upon their ability to consent.

Who do we call when there's no kiss, no nudity, no simulated sex, but when a Black body is cast as an enslaved person, or a non-Black body as an enslaver? Who do we call when a queer or Trans actor is asked to perform a gender that is not authentic to them? …Or when a hijabi is asked to simulate having to remove the headscarf from their head? Who holds space for the experience of disabled actors? ...Of spiritual and religious communities? ... Of survivors?

In some cases, intimacy professionals with specializations in those areas would be more than equipped to hold space for that type of story. In other cases, our entertainment industry has seen calls for change that have specifically called for professionals on set and stage who are trained in closing those systemic gaps.

The Origin of the Cultural Competency Professional

On June 8, 2020, at 7:00 pm EST, a collective called We See You, White American Theater (WSYWAT) released a call to action entitled "Dear White American Theater" outlining a specific list of injustices and demands for change from the greater American theatrical industry. They outlined a vision for change that included regular cultural competency trainings for industry professionals, updated codes of conducts for theaters that include policies on anti-racism and other anti-discrimination, resources for accountability as it pertains to race-based harm and active, actionable practices for when global majority artists and stories are inevitably invited into performance spaces. And, as the global industry followed suit, rattling under the calls for change, out of the rubble rose the cultural competency professional as a dedicated role on creative teams all over the world.

Around this time, pioneers in our industry put a name to a role that global majority artists have found themselves taking on, unacknowledged, for decades. Some artists have trademarked their own titles for the role such as "cultural coordinator" trademarked to Tavia Riveé Jefferson or "sensitivity specialist" trademarked to Ann James. I, myself, have taken on the role under the title of "cultural sensitivity director" and "cultural competency director", among others. However, no matter the title we dawn, the work remains the same.

Defining the Role

The scope of cultural competency specialist, similar to that of the intimacy professional, depends heavily on the production and the needs of the creative team and cast. In some productions, they may have a strong influence on the devising process, assisting the directing, dramaturgy and other creative and technical departments to curate creative and technical elements that deeply consider cultural elements and community care. Often, this includes finding affirming ways to stage decades old works while considering the cultural knowledge of the present day. However, it can also include supporting the cast and creative team to tell new, diverse cultural stories in a way that uplifts and cares for the community, preserves authenticity and vulnerability for the cultural experience and that considers the experience of the audience.

To achieve this, they combine the tools of anti-racism and other anti-discrimination frameworks with the tools of dramaturgy and consent-based performance to hold space for the relevant cultural themes present within the show. The role also supports the curation of content warnings and works alongside intimacy professionals, directors, writers, designers and other members of the creative team to find the resources and support needed for all involved in the production process to feel safe enough to continue holistically embodying the work. This can look like assisting the intimacy professional with adding specific cultural elements to intimate moments or highlighting the ways in which certain underlying cultural power dynamics can show up in the choreography of intimate moments.

In this way, cultural competency professionals are vital to nearly all performance spaces where either the story or the artists bringing the story to life find themselves with questions around how to properly care for the experiences of underrepresented communities. This includes the experience of Black, Indigenous and People of Color (BIPOC), the queer and Trans* community, the kink/BDSM community, religious groups, the telling and/or retelling of mythology, historical events, or oral traditions as well as any stories depicting other traditionally dehumanized populations in our culture.

Acknowledging the Need for Accountability

Like all other theatrical and creative disciplines, the cultural competency director should be brought into the process as early as possible so as to provide these resources before harm has the opportunity to occur. Cultural competency acknowledges that we cannot easily rebuild our trust in the systems that were built upon a foundation of an unjust past. It acknowledges that we cannot automatically heal the harm to those with multiple marginalized identities in rehearsal spaces or on sets around the world. It acknowledges that there is real work to be done in the rewiring of our performance processes and that this restructuring is a necessary step to curating bravery on our sets and stages.

Cultural Competency acknowledges the need for accountability.

Accountability, as in resources for survivors who are currently working within systems that have oppressed them. As in, options for reconstructing relationships that have been severed by mistrust. As in, an acknowledgment of how trauma and power manifests itself and lingers in spaces, in bodies and in the work. As in, documentation of the process and checkpoints for repair that can allow survivors the space to compassionately witness change happen before their eyes. As in, active and sustainable processes for preventing future harms in a space that has already been flagged as unsafe.

Abusive structures like white supremacy, ableism, cissexism and other cultural shortcomings that have built a foundation in our industry all thrive in the lack of accountable and actionable steps for maintaining change. So, I'm calling us out. Like those before me, I'm using my voice one more time to call on the industry to consider the gaps and allow our people to fill them.

Our industry needs to invest in accountability.

It needs to invest in acknowledging the wholeness of what impacts consent. It needs to invest in the spaces where it fails, where intimacy professionals are not enough to support the full breadth of work and the artists that create it. And with that investment in cultural competency, our industry will be to taking its next, sustainable step toward finishing the work.

Intimacy and Violence
A Conversation

Moderated by Cristina (Cha) Ramos with Rachel Flesher, Eli Lynn and Siobhan Richardson

> Cha Ramos has been a dear friend of mine and collaborator for years. I so admire her brain and her artistry. In talking about the idea of bringing many voices together in the book, she suggested doing that for this chapter. Rather than a traditional essay style chapter on intimacy and violence, she brings you a conversation about it. She invited Siobhan Richardson, Eli Lynn and Rachel Flesher and said of them, "each of these professionals has made their mark on the worlds of both staged violence and staged intimacy with original ideas, years of training and mentor/menteeship, and lots of joy and passion for the betterment of both crafts."

CHA   I've been seeing a trend that assumes intimacy and fight professionals have the same skillset, and that they are especially interchangeable on (huge air quotes here) "smaller scale" moments: a shove, a kiss, etc. What are your thoughts on that?

SIOBHAN   Well, my first thought is that it's not correct. Early on there were a lot of people who were moving into intimacy from fight work because, in some ways, the skills, the approach to working with actors, the approach to being in the rehearsal space, that collaborative necessity, do have similarities. What isn't similar is that actors tend to approach intimacy and fights with different sets of fears and excitement, so the intimacy or the fight director does need to have a particular toolkit to facilitate the work.

ELI Because I have both toolkits, I do get pinged to do both often. But I worry it's because people want to save money, and I try very hard to stay on top of saying, "No, these are separate jobs. I have separate contracts for them. I will be paid fully for both of them."

SIOBHAN I will be credited as both the fight and intimacy director. That's important to me.

RACHEL There are too many incredible fight and intimacy directors out there to undercut either industry! The fact is: both art forms take a lot of time (and usually money) to be trained in. When productions assume a fight director will know how to intimacy direct or vice versa they inadvertently pressure the designer to potentially do something they are not comfortable doing, which could cause harm. The assumption also diminishes the importance of each position as a sovereign and specialized art form.

CHA I have had some earlier career intimacy directors mention that they feel like they need to know *some* stage combat techniques to choreograph more physical scenes of intimacy. Is there any cross-training that you think *should* happen?

RACHEL Ideally I think *all* fight directors and intimacy directors would be trained in consent practices, trauma-informed movement practices and intersectionality. We work with bodies in space, and understanding gender inclusivity practices, anti-racism, anti-ableism and neurodiversity (to name a few) are vital to honor and support the actors doing the work.

ELI And, fundamentally, the job is about storytelling through movement. If you don't have any specific movement training or vocabulary or ability to communicate that to actors, or even the ability to think in that way, then you're not actually doing a big chunk of the job.

SIOBHAN I do think intimacy practitioners should know basic hair pulls, shoves, falling to the ground, rolling…

ELI Things like weight sharing, shared action… these are things I get from fight training that are useful to intimacy as well, especially if you're doing something that is rougher or more athletic, when actors are relying on each other for a bit more physical safety.

CHA	Ultimately, though, it's not just about physical safety... an ice skater may know how to fall safely or a martial artist may know how to pull a punch, but without the storytelling part that you mentioned earlier, it's not communicating anything. So whether it's stage combat, narrative dance or clown, it's about finding training that helps develop both an awareness of the physical safeties of movement *and* the ability to read and create movement-based storytelling. Having that much also helps with knowing when you *don't* have the skills needed for a moment...
RACHEL	An excellent opportunity for collaboration and creativity – hiring a second designer who does have the needed skills if you don't. Admitting you need more knowledge is *not* a weakness.
SIOBHAN	I'm thinking of, for example, a scene of intense sexual violence, then you need someone who either has a full grasp of both specialties or you need two people in the room at the same time and clear negotiation between those two people about how they're going to collaborate on creating those scenes.
RACHEL	I find collaborating with fellow intimacy or violence directors exciting. I get to see how other designers like to work, I get to see how actors and design teams react to different forms of communication. Plus, the actors have more voices in the space so the power is spread out across more people. It offers space for more identities to be represented in the space. And it can lead to ideas that would not have occurred if I was working a job alone.
CHA	And yet, many of us do find ourselves doing both roles alone, and there are benefits and challenges to that.
SIOBHAN	One benefit I've found of being able to do both is that there are still a lot of old (bordering on harmful) and terrible-looking stage combat practices out there. So I've used people's desire for intimacy direction to help elevate the evolution of stage combat, or at least that's been my intention.
CHA	The practice of intimacy direction has certainly affected my fight practice, and vice versa. For me, getting to hold both movement styles in the same room can sometimes allow for a deeper continuity in the movement storytelling overall *as well as* continuity in how we're addressing the physical and psychological safety of the actors.
ELI	I will say if it's a really big ask, for either violence or intimacy or both, I think it's important to have the jobs separated. Like Rachel said, it's more voices in the room, and it means I have the

energy and the space to be keeping an eye more focused on one side or the other.

SIOBHAN Whoever is hiring needs to be really explicit about what they're hiring for. If it's a really robust scene of intimacy and people are shoving each other onto the bed or pushing each other to the walls, then I think it's advisable for the intimacy person to have that fight/action expertise.

CHA Or for there to be a separate fight director.

SIOBHAN Some industry education might be needed to clarify where the line is between intimacy and violence/action and where the crossover is, so that engagers can be clear about what role(s) they're actually hiring for. And if they expect this person to have skills of tossing people's bodies around, or if they want the violence to be intimate, then that needs to be explicit in the hiring process.

CHA This is where phrases like "intimate violence" and "violent intimacy" become important to define. What do they mean to you?

SIOBHAN I tend to use "violent intimacy" to describe scenes of a more sexual nature with, for lack of better clarity, a hard edge. I also sometimes call it athletic intimacy or robust intimacy or active intimacy, e.g. people are making out and pushing each other into walls, getting to the floor very quickly, etc.

ELI Scenes of sexual assault obviously fall in this category for me. But there is a spectrum of particularly physical intimacy – with consensual but rough play on one end, and a scene of violent sexual assault on the other. And I see an even subtler version of violent intimacy as intimacy that has a really clear power dynamic.

RACHEL The primary throughline for "violent intimacy" for me is that the act is an intimate act first that has the quality of violence. While when I think of "intimate violence" the throughline for me is that it is a violent act first that has the quality of intimacy; violence that is heightened by something exceedingly vulnerable. I place non-consensual intimacy in both categories because there is a wide range of non-consensual intimate scenes. Intimate violence has also begun to mean domestic violence in my vocabulary, and that does not need to be physical to be devastating…

CHA There are even certain styles of fighting that can just *feel* more intimate because they are closer contact and/or more familiar to people (knife fighting, fighting with found objects, etc.) Most people know what it feels like to get cut with a kitchen knife, so as actors fighting with a knife or as an audience witnessing a knife fight, we have a direct personal relationship to that object.

ELI   And with found objects you have a creative choice to *make it* more intimate. If we use certain objects in a moment of violence (a treasured journal in a fight between sisters in *The Moors*, for example), then our relationship to those things emotionally, as the audience and as the characters, can make it more intimate.

CHA   I think that's why I bring these terms up in relation to Siobhan's point about hiring the right professional(s). Depending on the quality of the scene, you might need an intimacy professional with some amount of staged violence training, a fight professional with some amount of staged intimacy training, or two professionals who are each responsible for one whole aspect of the movement's sustainability and storytelling.

SIOBHAN   And with the kind of intimacy and violence we're talking about, it's so important to embed the idea that on one plane of this work it is simply choreography repeated, even if it's very simple choreography. If you're not "feeling it" one night in the show, that's totally fine. It's not about feeling it. It's about what the audience perceives and the audience's experience of it. And I find that really helps to put our focus on: what's the story for the audience? And how are we, the performers and the creators, doing that sustainably?

CHA   On that note: what other tools or concepts from your work would you especially like to share?

SIOBHAN   I always start with communication. Something I learned from Matt Richardson was that communication is our number one safety, and that continues to hold true with everything that we do. Let the team know when we're going to start vocalizing, when we're running it just as pure movement, etc. We don't have to do these moments with the full context of the character every time. And we shouldn't be. It's too exhausting on the system to put ourselves into our sympathetic state all the time. Sometimes we just need to work out movement, timing, placement. I try to remind actors that it doesn't have to hurt them to be good work.

CHA   It can even be *fun*!

ELI   We've been talking quite a bit about scenes that blur between violence and intimacy but sometimes they're very distinct, so I've started lovingly using the term "an Intimus" to mean a discrete moment of intimacy, like: "this is the Intimus, here, I can hold it in my hand!" as opposed to something that could blur the lines or that spills out into more of the action of the play.

CHA	I'm imagining an enemies-to-lovers swashbuckling sword fight with one passionate kiss thrown in somewhere – an "Intimus" in an otherwise silly fight scene!
RACHEL	The intersection of violence and intimacy has *endless* possibilities and applications. It is so exciting to watch both industries grow and flourish with ideas and the introduction of new and seasoned practitioners.
SIOBHAN	I also think it's important to name that, when we hold both skill sets, we may not only be supporting movement and consent in these moments, but also contextual historical and cultural consultation, the use of distance and proximity and body language in storytelling, sustainable and impactful voice work, and more!
CHA	And we don't need to be experts in all those things, but we do need to be able to facilitate those conversations as they pertain to moments of violence and/or intimacy, and encourage the team to invite in other experts as needed (cultural consultants, dramaturgs, vocal coaches) to create those moments collaboratively.
RACHEL	Ultimately each individual (and team) deserves the space to dictate what they deem as violent or intimate or hyper-exposed, and what support they need. Danger lies in the white-supremacist, patriarchal, capitalist, heteronormative, cis-centered, colonizer scripts that we have been fed on what "should" be called vulnerable and what "should not" be.
SIOBHAN	The way forward is for us all to take responsibility for our workplaces and to invite qualified professionals to help us whenever possible.
ELI	I always say: ask me anything. I can't always answer the question or fix the problem for you, but I will talk to somebody about it for you, because in this vulnerable work people come to us with things they may be nervous to ask anybody else. It makes me think of the spectrum from uncomfortable to unsafe. I want actors to feel empowered to be uncomfortable, but I never want them to feel unsafe. If you only ever do things with which you're 100 percent comfortable, you're less likely to make daring stories and you're less likely to grow as an artist. That said, I'm not going to choreograph a fight, for example, that is right up against your physical limits, and the same is true for intimacy.
CHA	It's our responsibility to create choreography – whether violent, intimate, or both – that tells the story truthfully and allows our actors to do daring work within that choreography in a way that is healthy and sustainable.

Mental Health Coordination

Amanda Edwards with contribution from Bridget McCarthy

> When the intimacy industry first gained prominence, there were folks saying that, in order to be an intimacy professional, one must have mental health first aid. I agree with that; quite frankly, I think everyone should have mental health first aid training. However, it seemed to me that some folks heard that suggested requirement and took it to mean that Ips were responsible for the mental safety of the creative team. Once that idea got planted, no matter how many people in positions of authority said, "we are not mental health practitioners," I still found that there were directors and producers coming into meetings with me with the wrong impression of our scope of practice. Some novice intimacy professionals, with very good intentions, were inserting themselves into situations where they weren't qualified, further confusing the issue. So, here's the thing: we do sometimes need mental health professionals in theatre, TV and film and the intimacy industry emerged at a time when the arts industry was waking up to issues of care and sustainability. The good news is that there is a position that fills that need.
>
> Amanda Edwards is a mental health professional and intimacy coordinator. She and Bridget McCarthy saw this area of need and co-founded the Association of Mental Health Coordinators. I asked Amanda to write about the role of mental health coordinators and how they are different from and work with intimacy professionals.

Mental health coordinators (MHCs) are mental health professionals and entertainment artists who use tools from both fields to support inclusive, compelling and ethical storytelling.

This breaks down as follows

Mental health professionals: We are trained as mental health professionals beyond crisis counseling or Mental Health First Aid. Though many of us are licensed social workers, counselors or therapists, all of us have shared training in trauma, attachment, core human needs, stabilization, assessment and ethical referrals. We also have an expectation of cultural competency and a practice of continuing education and rigorous training or experience requirements. We value evidence, practice-based and lived experience work in both the clinical and artistic setting.

Entertainment artists: Most have a background in theatre, film, dance, opera, technical artistry or other spaces, which brings a shared vocabulary from all artistic backgrounds.

Inclusive, compelling and ethical storytelling: mental health coordinators work for rigorous and compelling storytelling, both for the creators and the consumers. We acknowledge that good intentions are not enough ethically, especially about such sensitive topics as trauma, mental health crises or substance use challenges so we work to "skill up" creative spaces to tell these stories in ways that reduce harm and promote healing for both creators and consumers. For example, we might work with an organization telling a story of suicide by crafting a care network within the production, and also cultivating the audience experience with resources and deroling exercises. We might work on a film that has nothing to do with mental health in the story, but instead serve a production company struggling with power dynamics and conflict, which needs support there. Wholeheartedly, we believe that by investing in ethical practices we can tell stories that are even more interesting, complex and potentially healing for everyone involved.

We acknowledge that the work of mental health and intimacy professionals lives within a spectrum that is not always clear, and in which binary labels are not always helpful in getting individuals and organizations the support that they need. With that in mind, we have begun the process of creating a spectrum of duties that lie closer to one role or another. Determining one's place within this spectrum is an ethical responsibility and can only be determined, ultimately, by the individual practitioner.

What we do

We specialize in working in spaces that are high tension and high potential for conflict or trauma.

- Choreograph scenes that contain potentially traumatic material.
- Assess a script or project for hot spots (a risk analysis).
- Make recommendations of or for responsible, compelling portrayal of trauma, substance use or mental health challenges.
- Support actors not hurting themselves through lots of tools from first audition to a project wrap (which might include decompressing from the work).
- Supervise, support and advocate for the wellbeing of minors involved in a project.
- Help keep audiences safer with appropriate media guidelines and content disclosures.
- Act as first responder to mental health crises within an artistic space (like a set medic but for mental health).
- Support conflict and concern navigation.
- Provide training and policy support to companies and organizations to infuse more mental health awareness into their practices.

While it's true that many intimacy professionals are trained in choreography and the portrayal of traumatic material, training in supporting a performer whose life experience mirrors that same trauma is missing. While training as an IP may include Mental Health First Aid, there is no understanding of symptom profiles for diagnoses and how to portray them responsibly.

> While there is an increase in awareness of trauma informed practices in the world of intimacy, there's no ethical way an intimacy professional can be expected to be a qualified mental health coordinator!

What we Don't do

We don't treat mental illness or solve all of a company's problems.

Ultimately, the job of the MHC is to help support care across the board. We utilize the Salutogenic Standards to outline that for ourselves and our clients. With immense gratitude to the intimacy movement, we work beyond consent and focus on the expectations outlined below. These standards help us ensure that we are working ethically, beyond consent. Consent is just a part of the equation in how *we* define care. We want to invest in a culture of care according to the Salutogenic Standards as follows:.

- Consent: informed, reversible, embodied or enthusiastic, specific.
- Coordination of work: clear communication between all parties involved.
- Information and education: access to relevant information across an entire team.
- Physical safety and comfort: safe and secure working conditions for everyone.
- Accessibility and access to care: individuals have access to tools they can use themselves as well as supports to meet their access needs.
- Attachment to community: parties experience attachment and value in community and with one another, work/life balance is encouraged.

Liability

Misrepresentation of scope of practice is not only dangerous to the folks under our care, but could also result in personal liability. Intimacy professionals are now starting to understand the need for insurance, but policies will not cover a professional operating outside of their professional areas of expertise. We encourage all professionals to reflect on their training and education as well as lived experience in order to determine what projects and environments they're most qualified to support.

The question of "scope of practice" has been boiled down in the intimacy world to a question of "qualification and certification." However, reducing the question of "who can do what work" is not served by a simple binary, and requires a great deal more nuance, self-assessment, support, accountability and experience. Scope of practice is designed to be freeing, not limiting. It frees the practitioner to focus on their speciality, rather than attempting to be all things for all projects.

> We offer the RECITE acronym to support professionals to examine their areas of expertise within a given project or role, briefly summarized here:
>
> **Role:** what professional and personal "hat" is worn and has everyone consented to it?

Environment: what is the relationship to this space and is it ready for my presence? Have I assessed and communicated expectations and boundaries?

Cultural competency: do I understand the nuances of this culture / am I *really* the right person for this job?

(Conflict of) interest: is there a reason to *not* do this work? What could I gain / others gain from me?

Training: do I have the necessary training to do this? Does someone else have more training?

Experience: do I have hands-on experience doing this or do I have a lifeline to access someone who has?

Where do we go from here?

We sincerely believe that the future holds collaboration between intimacy professionals and mental health coordinators, in order to truly best support the health and wellness of productions *while* simultaneously creating movement and moments to tell the stories that matter most.

Introduction to Part Two

Specialities

Brooke M. Haney

Part Two will dive into some of the specialties that exist within the industry. I asked intimacy professionals whose work I admire and respect to write in their voice from their experience in an area in which they specialize. I've asked them to write their chapters to ICs who might specialize in their subject, rather than to all ICs. So, don't be surprised if there is a certain level of knowledge assumed in a chapter. If you are an IC or an IC in training, I hope you will find a chapter that calls to you and helps you to clarify where you might specialize. If you are a director or producer, I hope that reading these chapters will help you to understand some of the different specialties that exist and in doing so will aid you in evaluating a project and more effectively interviewing intimacy professionals.

Each chapter in Part Two could (and should) have its own book. However, most of them had to be written in less than 2,000 words. As such, they can't possibly cover everything or even all the most important things about their given specialty. These chapters are meant to whet your palate for more. Some have resources listed at the end, and even these resources are just a jumping off point.

Some of the specialties are overarching and have lots of subspecialties. For example, Olivia "Troy" Troy writes on BDSM, for which she is an incredible expert. That chapter is followed by an interview with kink expert Midori and a chapter co-written by Megan Gilron and me on scenes involving rope. BDSM and kink are only restrained by the imagination and yet they have so little representation and even less positive, realistic representation in the media.

Similarly, I give a brief overview of tools and techniques for working on stories involving trauma, and Amy Northup goes into greater detail on how to apply tools more specifically on scenes involving sexual trauma or non-consent. By honing in on this topic, we hope to provide deeper learning that can be translated to other specialties as well.

Our queer chapter is limited to T4T, lesbian and gay male sex. This leaves out much of the vastness of gender expressions, non-monogamy, group sex dynamics, queerness and kink, not to mention intersections of race and disability. Not all of these are exclusive to queer relationships, and they do often connect with queer relationships in ways that deserve accurate thoughtful storytelling.

Despite the fact that these chapters are brief and often general, I asked the writers to be as specific as possible. I believe the more specific writers are, the more universally applicable their thoughts. Kaja Dunn, for example, writes on Black American Intimacy, but no one writes specifically on intimacy considerations for other races. I'm hoping that by looking at Kaja's chapter, someone can see areas that should be considered when working with other stories of race or culture and research, read, take classes or hire a consultant to fill in the examples.

No one talks in-depth in this book about the dangers of assuming white as default when talking about race. As you read, be mindful to not assume whiteness in the specialties. With each specialty, consider what other specialties intersect with it, and, before trying to specialize in one area, make sure to have competency in areas such as race, gender and sexuality, disability, etc. with an eye to intersection.

Between chapters, I have included conversations I had with actors, directors, writers and producers who have worked with intimacy coordinators. These interludes are here to give anecdotes and examples of the different ways ICs can work. Some of these are directly connected to specialties discussed and some are simply stories I found insightful and valuable.

There are so many specialties that I wish I could have included in this book and there wasn't nearly enough room. As the industry continues to grow and our practice continues to evolve, I hope there is a second, third and fourth volume.

Things to Consider

For intimacy professionals

- Do any of these specialties particularly excite me?
- What strengths or knowledge do I already possess?
- What learning do I still have to do and where can I do it?

For directors and producers

- How do I break down my projects when I think about hiring an intimacy professional?
- Does my project include any of these specialties?

For Actors

- What kinds of roles am I cast in often?
- What roles do I hope to play or projects do I hope to work on?
- Are there any skills around self care or boundaries setting that I can work on now to prepare me for this type of work?

International Considerations

6

Cessalee Stovall

> Cessalee Stovall is an artist, intimacy director and coordinator, cultural consultant and an equity, access and inclusion specialist, with a focus on the performing arts sector. Cessalee is an unapologetic champion for the physical, psychological and cultural safety of all humans in our industry. She is the founder and director of Stage A Change, an organization that works to increase, amplify and sustain professional opportunities for artists of colour in Australia. I met Cessalee when she was traveling on a grant, doing research in the intimacy industry, and was excited by her approach to our work. I knew her experience would make her a wonderful choice to talk about considerations when working internationally.

I'm an American born and trained actor, who moved to Australia to study intimacy direction from a New Yorker and a Brit. As I navigated the road between certification, dynamic learning opportunities and channeling my own practice as an artist and advocate, ultimately my praxis as an intimacy professional has been informed through international experiences viewed through my Black American/Australian lens. My core beliefs about the most effective and impactful way to support cultural and psychological safety comes down to this – listen and learn to lift. That mantra applies specifically to my work in film, TV and theatre as an intimacy professional, but also to the way I show up in spaces around the world, simultaneously as an insider and outsider.

Listen and Learn To Lift

As I continue to deepen my understanding of safety and advocacy in my work, it has become clear to me that my first task is to be present in the space, celebrating the expertise of self I'm surrounded by. I have to start by listening with all senses – I hear the people, I feel the energy, I consider the community, I respect the culture around me in order to absorb or learn as much as I can. My positionality, whether as an insider or outsider, will always be informed by the project and players and this critical step must proceed "the work." By adding the extra step of listening to learn, I remind myself of the context I'm working within, decentering my "knowledge" to make space for the missing information that will inform my practice. It is at this point that I'm able to do "the work" in response to what I've heard and what I've learned. I am now able to consider how I might lift or elevate the working agreements, the mechanisms of safety and fully advocate for the best possible performance.

While I feel lucky to have personal experience of working in multiple countries and with people who are working outside of their home country, I do not begin to imagine I can be an expert on all people and cultures. In my years of experience both as an intimacy professional and as an equity and inclusion facilitator, it's been a privilege to have access to spaces where I can listen to the needs and experiences of artists, learn how to provide support for them and ultimately uplift and empower them in their work and process. When working to listen and learn, I stay keenly attentive to **culture, industry and practice**.

Culture

Addressing and actioning protocols for cultural safety vary greatly based on country and individual practices. Cultural norms and expectations are a crucial consideration for any interactions on set or in rehearsal, and it's imperative that the directors and the intimacy team are addressing not only the norms and expectations of the actors, but also of the characters. For example, in some countries, theatre dressing rooms are traditionally mixed genders – in other places that would not be appropriate. In consideration of non-binary and Trans identities and bodies, it's particularly important to be tuned into stage management and venue conversations, and even more so if the production will tour to other venues. In some contexts, like some Latinx communities, or a familial or end-of-life context, touching someone's head or hair is a sign of endearment. In other cultures that could be on the border of fetishization, i.e., a person wearing a hijab, or a Black person with natural hair being touched by someone outside of that group. In a few places, it is inappropriate for any person to touch the top of someone's head without being a spouse, as in New Zealand with Māori culture. One note, I give these and later specific examples with a caveat – as with any boundary, these same norms can vary, even amongst people of the same background, culture and nationality.

> No group should be considered a monolith. While it would not be expected for any person to know every cultural norm in a country, creating space for the context of cultural protocols to inform the choreography is imperative.

Beyond general considerations in culture, there can be a difference in understanding of how consent intersects with culture. A common example would be on greeting. In the US, a handshake or hug would be an expected way to meet a stranger. In Canada or Italy, that might also include a kiss in the air, near or on the cheek. In some places, for example certain East Asian countries, the most respectful way to engage would be by keeping some distance. As an intimacy professional, understanding the cultural norms around touch is quite useful when prepping artists and directors in initial calls. And beyond the expectations of greetings, the variance in expectation of consent vary by nationality. Each of the aforementioned greetings could easily be executed with an expectation of consent based on the cultural norms surrounding them. Considering the potential impact of this initial engagement, IPs must include both in performance and non-performance-based considerations into our boundary discussions to help equip artists with information, especially when they may be feeling like a geographic outsider.

When working in a global context, IPs should also consider the demographics of the audience: who has access physically, financially and contextually to engage with the work and how they will experience it in relation to their own lived experience. In film and TV, it is important to understand who the audience is and how they will view this work. Creating an intimate scene between a Black and white interracial couple in the US is wildly different than those same bodies set in Ghana, or China. The demographics of the country adds context to the story and sometimes, particularly in theatre, a different context for your audiences. If an audience does not historically see certain bodies in society, or on stage, there is a likelihood that the audience will first see that human as part of the "out group," before they accept that person as part of the story. In other words, intimacy professionals are well served to consider how the demographics of the community, who will engage with this work as audience, will recognize the bodies onstage, based on their own knowledge and access to those identities. More than "how much does this audience know about these characters" it becomes "what is the impact of telling this story with these humans to these people?"

For example, I was working on a recent production that included a dynamic kissing scene with a Black male performer and a white female performer. Considering the historic perceptions of Black male bodies in the country, the impact on Australian audiences seeing a Black man actively, albeit playfully, push a white girl down to kiss has a much more exoticized context than it would have in the US, where interracial relationships are more common and there are comparatively a higher percentage of Black men in society. Conversely, had it been an Aboriginal male actor with a white female actor, I would need to consider pervasive and harmful stereotypes of the primitive and devious nature of Aboriginal people in Australian media (Briscoe, 2020).

Industry

The global response to intimacy direction and intimacy work has been swift. Access to training, a robust industry and large scale productions with increased demand (or request) by actors, directors and production have led to exponential growth in the field in the US and UK. But countries like South Africa, India, Canada, Australia and New Zealand, rich with their own film, TV and theatre productions, have seen a much more measured increase both in personnel and uptake. It is unlikely that these slower-to-rise numbers are the result of knowledge or interest, but more likely simply due to the size and processes of the industry, which can vary greatly from country to country. Nations with a smaller industry are more dependent on word of mouth and in-network connections, which has considerable bearing on professionals trying to break into an industry without a clear entry point.

> In countries that are smaller or have more close-knit industries, the reliance on word of mouth and reputation are important factors for job security.

Networks become critical for sustainability, and the likelihood of harm for artists and interruption of process is often exponentially tied to the number of outsiders on a project. While many productions are prepared to take that risk, awareness of the hierarchies and working agreements in a new place will often accelerate the speed of trust from those on the inside.

Both theatre and film/TV industries have different languages in different parts of the world, even amongst English-speaking countries. In the US, it's stage right and left, in Australia, it's prompt side and opposite prompt side. Places is beginners, a cowboy shot is an American shot, clocking your scene partner is either looking at them or hitting them. In addition to the vernacular, the systems of support vary greatly as you move across the globe. The presence and enforcement power of the unions and guilds have a great impact on the way live performance and film and TV is made. It's impractical to assume the same protections or operations apply country to country, and specifically intimacy professionals should ensure they are confident on the regulations of the country (and the assumptions of international artists) with regards to children's working rights, age and legality of consent, working hours for talent and crew, harassment and bullying regulations, audition protocols, riders and legal language. So…

Practice

There are a few things to keep in mind while in production. In broad strokes, the first step of building cultural safety is critical self-reflection. Start by examining your practice to determine your positionality in the space. Assess and address any identity-based biases or blind spots you might have and maintain an awareness of the politics (if any) that your presence presents in the space. Colonization and qualification have brought about the notion that works that originate from the US or UK are the works, or working styles, that are most worthy of replication and recognition. Consider if your expectations and process are furthering that myth and identify how you might lift the culture instead of minimizing it.

> As more and more countries investigate their pathways to decolonization, it's important to address your proximity to power (imbalance) based on your nationality or the place you learned or honed your skills.

When on set, avoid assumptions about roles, responsibilities and hierarchies based on your home country's protocols. Outside the English-speaking world quite often the roles and set functions can vary quite a bit. In India, the caste system is very much at play and can overshadow Anglo-centric role hierarchies as per the flow chart. Particularly in countries where the intimacy director or coordinator's role is not fully developed, an intimacy professional is often not addressed as a head of department, but instead as an assistant or support role. Though sometimes you may be working for a production company you are familiar with (i.e. Netflix), the partners, local producing house or individual producers may have a different idea of how to operate. Remaining agile and collaborative in those moments will smooth out your process on set.

Once you have worked through all (or some) of the above, the actual practice will become clearer for you. Working in consideration of the culture of the industry, artists and audiences will give you a framework for engagement, enabling you to better advocate for and uplift the artists.

One final consideration is for the artist process. Particularly in markets where intimacy direction is new and/or showing intimacy on stage, film or TV is a relatively new idea, there should be considerations of the closure practices for artists and the consideration of post-production trauma. In 2022, a program in South Africa found itself as a hot topic after intimate scenes between two characters were described as pornography on social media. The assumption of the audiences that intercourse occurred, the cultural implications of the actors being intimate with people who were not their partners, and the professional stigma meant that in addition to defending their craft as actors via an unexpected press junket, they needed to defend their work and their integrity publicly. This level of emotional and psychological stress on artists is particularly common when intimacy direction is in some ways still undefined in the industry and unfamiliar to audiences. In this case, the actors went to the press to demystify the intimacy and clarify the boundaries and barriers in place. This sort of explosive reaction is not unique to one country. For example, India – where historically sex has been alluded to with images like flowers, an unmade bed or a sunset – requires another level of closure consideration as the end of the filming is not always the end of the impact or participation. Additional support may be required through the editing, publicity or marketing, and release stages. Intimacy professionals are well placed to liaise with producers to consider the resources necessary to navigate public response, personal and reputational harm, and career impact, especially for young artists. Closure technique might include giving the artists language to address criticism, media talking points or other re-humanizing techniques to bring the artist out of character impact and back to self. As some of these supports sit outside the scope of the intimacy professional, ideally this closure is in collaboration with other departments like the PR and marketing teams.

Working in an international context can be thrilling and exciting. The cultural and professional considerations cannot be underestimated and their significance for the artists, crew, audiences and the producers is highlighted when working from a decolonized framework. It is then crucial, as intimacy professionals, that we take on a decentered lens, acknowledge the effects of our presence and practice and remain mindful of the cultural differences, learn industry expectations and understand the artist impact that comes with international work to ensure our engagement is effective, respectful and uplifting.

Bibliography

Bhattacharya, Bina. Interview. Conducted by Cessalee Stovall. February 3, 2023.

Briscoe, Luke. "Racism in media provides a blockage for Indigenous prosperity in a digital economy." SBS. August 31, 2020. https://www.sbs.com.au/nitv/article/racism-in-media-provides-a-blockage-for-indigenous-prosperity-in-a-digital-economy/3n0syvqmh.

Hilton, Emily. "Let's Talk About Simulated Sex: Intimacy Coordinators Two Years On." The Hollywood Reporter. December 10, 2020. https://www.hollywoodreporter.com/tv/tv-news/lets-talk-about-simulated-sex-intimacy-coordinators-two-years-on-4101799/.

Lush, Kate. Interview. Conducted by Cessalee Stovall. February 16, 2023.

van den Heever, Megan. "The Wife sex scene: Khanyi Mbau spills the tea on what really happened." The South African. March 15, 2022. https://www.thesouthafrican.com/lifestyle/celeb-news/breaking-the-wife-sex-scene-zansile-nkosana-khanyi-mbau-mondli-makhoba/.

A Conversation with Nesta Cooper

Brooke M. Haney

> Nesta Cooper and I first worked together on the film *Turn Me On* directed by Michael Tyburski. From our first meeting, Michael told me that his priority was for the actors to feel safe and know that they could always withdraw consent. So, I met with the actors individually to talk through their scenes and get, from them, the language for their riders. The first time I met with Nesta was on Zoom, and I was really excited by her ability to articulate her boundaries very specifically. She basically mapped out her body and clarified inch by inch what would work for her. This impressed me and I found that throughout our work together, as things changed in the film, Nesta was able to check in with herself and let me know where she was at day to day.

BROOKE   We worked together in 2022 on *Turn Me On*. Had you worked with an intimacy coordinator before that?

NESTA   I had worked with three intimacy coordinators actually. Two times were in Canada, and I always feel like Canada is a bit more innovative in terms of being very respectful around intimacy.

BROOKE   Yeah, currently the rules for ACTRA, the Canadian actor's union, are in fact different and more protective than the rules of SAG/AFTRA, the American actor's union.

DOI: 10.4324/9781003410553-10

NESTA   ACTRA is not great in terms of protecting its workers in comparison to SAG, money-wise and stuff, but for some reason, intimacy is taken very seriously there, so I feel really lucky that I haven't had a ton of bad experiences.

BROOKE   Can you talk about an experience you've had with an IC that was complicated?

NESTA   Leading up to this one scene there were multiple discussions. The intimacy coordinator had storyboarded everything, which was so helpful to me. I really like to just know everything. That makes me feel the most comfortable. I feel like it gives me space to work within to try to feel my most beautiful and confident, if that's what the scene calls for. I really wanted to make sure that myself and my scene partner felt very safe.

BROOKE   That sounds like a great start. What changed that made it complicated?

NESTA   It was almost like when we got to the day, it was like walking on eggshells, and no one wanted to talk about the fact that we were doing the scene, people wanted to just pretend like it was just a normal day, including the intimacy coordinator. So when it got down to actually doing the scene, I felt extremely uncomfortable because I was sitting there basically naked with this woman, who also didn't have as much experience as me, and people were just kind of just avoidant, wouldn't look near or even close to us. And it was just one of the most uncomfortable experiences I've ever been in. It's kind of hard to describe why that is, because it's not like I was being violated in any way.

BROOKE   Then, the director needed to change the original plan for the scene, right?

NESTA   Yeah, and I think where I really felt failed was that the director was hiding in another room. And he refused to come in and speak to us. And the intimacy coordinator was so scared of the director that she didn't want to say anything either. So no one was really directing the scene, and then it just was so awkward.

BROOKE   How did you find support?

NESTA   Afterwards, I called my manager. He was like "where was the showrunner? Why wasn't there anybody on set? Let me just talk to everyone and figure this out." And that was very validating, because after that, I got a call from our female exec, I got a call from our showrunner, and I got taken aside and spoken to and apologized to by the director the next day. It was just very validating, because they basically were like, "look, you're right, we all were so freaked out. The director was so freaked out about doing the wrong thing, he didn't want to go in and talk to you because he didn't want to upset you, because he knew he had already changed the scene." And I was like "listen, I get that but I still need to feel like I'm being directed or I'm not going to feel confident."

I wasn't, before, the kind of actor that would call my team. I really do recommend that you do that, because that's what they're there for. If you have a team that cares about you, they know the right people to talk to, to kind of sort things out. That was very, very validating for me.

BROOKE I'm really glad your manager supported you in that way.

NESTA Also, being in America in this very kind of divided air, it adds to the tension, people just not wanting to say the wrong thing, get canceled. It feels so simple when you're in my position, to just be normal and nice, and don't say weird things. But, I can also understand someone's perspective, so it's tricky.

BROOKE It's interesting, on one hand, the industry has tons of experience staging scenes of intimacy. And on the other hand, working with intimacy coordinators is relatively new. In the long run, it will be an abundantly positive thing, **and** there are some learning moments happening right now that may involve a little fragility. When a director's, producer's or crew's thoughts are occupied by not wanting to be perceived as offensive or needing folks to understand that they are good people, it can get in the way of clear communication. How do you think a director, who is nervous, should approach working on scenes of intimacy?

NESTA I think that filmmakers, especially male filmmakers, when working with women, need to feel more comfortable with being uncomfortable and being wrong, and being open to maybe saying the wrong thing, but coming from a place of learning and humility. It's just such a fine line between people being afraid of offending someone to just treating someone like a human being.

BROOKE Okay, what advice would you give to an early career actor who was doing a scene of intimacy for their first time?

NESTA Break down the script and try to understand how the intimacy moves the story along, and what it means to your character emotionally. And then from there, assuming that it's a consensual, intimate scene, really think about what you feel like you're most comfortable doing, like actually take the time to really meditate on it, try to visualize how you can imagine you would look. And then do everything you can to make sure that you feel confident, beautiful and sexy.

I think that that starts with the costume, speaking with hair and makeup, covering up anything that you need and doing everything that you can to just feel very much in your body and confident in yourself. Because if you can walk onto the set with your head high, you're going to make a lot of really good decisions for yourself. And then, of course, don't be afraid to speak up and say what you need and trust your director, hopefully, if you can. And, speak with your scene partner. Just feel like you're having a fun, collaborative experience.

Now it would be separate advice, if it was an assault or rape scene. Which I have done. What helped me with doing a scene like that was I spoke with the intimacy coordinator about my boundaries in terms of what made me feel uncomfortable. You have to find a balance between how you're going to be able to do the scene emotionally, but also, you don't want to traumatize yourself for real life, right?

BROOKE   Yes, when we put our bodies in the positions or the shapes of fear, grief, etc., they don't know that we're playing pretend. What works or doesn't work for you in these types of scenes?

NESTA   I had a very bad trigger with being pinned down, especially in the chest area. And I had thought, before we started filming the scene, it would be good if the other actor pinned me down, because it really brought out this visceral reaction in me. That intimacy coordinator was like, "I really don't suggest doing that." And I'm really glad that she said that, because I think any person, if they're put in that position, will still feel like they're being attacked.

My advice to any actors would be to really, really take care of your heart and your brain. And remember that your body does not know that you're acting, if it feels like it's in stress, or it's in danger. Those chemicals will stay in your body, it doesn't know that it's not real life. So make sure that you know exactly how many takes you want to do of the very intense stuff. Be like, "I think I can only do this three times," so that they can cut around it or stop before or whatever. You just do whatever you need to do in the morning: pray, journal. You know, talk to your body, tell it it's safe. Take as many breaks as you can.

BROOKE   After working on something like that, what do you do to come back to Nesta? Do you have a ritual or personal closure practice?

NESTA   I always take a bath. I usually will go home, I'll take a bath with Epsom salts, and I listen to music. And if I'm feeling really like a shell of myself, I'll even put rose petals in the bath, just a little something for me. Some nice smelling oils, light candles, all this is my favorite closure practice. And I usually watch my favorite show. You know, just really, really pampering myself. It's my favorite thing to do.

Working with Minors 7

Kim Shively

> Many years ago, when I was working at a college, I got pushback for encouraging the department to introduce the tenets of intimacy professionals in the first year acting and directing programs. They said that they thought the students were too young and needed that year to adapt to college life, choosing to start that training in the second year. This boggled my mind. No one is too young to learn to consider and advocate for their boundaries, and creating a consent-forward classroom should be at the forefront of any arts program. Kim Shively works with minors as an intimacy choreographer and coordinator professionally and in academia. She is a professor and consults for several K–12 schools. So, I thought she was an ideal person to speak on this topic.

Content note: this chapter will include a discussion about the sexual exploitation and distribution of nude photos of underage performers.

For an intimacy coordinator, the concept of understanding and adhering to a scope of practice, or working within one's lane, can be extremely helpful. I find that this principle becomes essential when working with minors. Minors are designated by the law, and supporting the minor and their guardian, as well as the director's vision and production, may require specific considerations. Additionally, knowledge of what factors have gone into

DOI: 10.4324/9781003410553-11

determining how the law classifies minors, and how neurocognitive development plays a role in the perception of consent and boundaries, can help shape an IC's approach. While being an "expert" in minors is not necessary to work effectively with minors, there are ways to ensure an ethical and effective approach.

When the actors involved in the production are minors, there are additional considerations that the IC should be ready and able to communicate clearly as part of this scope of practice. It is important to think about **developmental psychology** and how often the law falls short of understanding what makes someone the age of majority, or able to fully consent. An IC must also be versed in **legal aspects of minors on set** and be ready to advocate for an optimal outcome for all involved in the production process with the minor's well-being centered.

At the time of writing this chapter, actors Olivia Hussey and Leonard Whiting are suing Paramount Pictures for "sexually exploiting them and distributing nude images of adolescent children," in the critically acclaimed production of Franco Zeffirelli's *Romeo and Juliet* (Maddaus, 2023). At the time of the production, Hussey was 15 and Whiting was 16. The stars allege that they were led to believe the film would fail if they were not nude in the now famous bedroom scene, which shows Hussey's breasts and Whiting's buttocks. The intricacies of this case demonstrate how trust in a director and process, coupled with the culture of "saying yes to anything regardless of one's boundaries," creates environments where consent for minors is more complicated than what first meets the eye.

Laws Regarding Minors

When looking to the law, the issue of consent and minors becomes even more complicated. In the United States, the Federal Government recognizes a minor as anyone under the age of 18, an age where one legally assumes adulthood with all its rights and responsibilities. This was ultimately determined by a variety of factors including military conscription, voting rights and science's limited understanding of brain development during the twentieth century (Lai, 2023).

When considering the most recent research published from the Annie E Casey Foundation's report on brain development (2023), in their resource guide, *The Road to Adulthood: Aligning Child Welfare Practice with Adolescent Brain Development*, it becomes clear that the cognitive development associated with adulthood can happen as late as the early thirties.

If we couple this information with an understanding of the trauma response of fawn, we then can gather how, years later, actors emerge from childhood with lawsuits that address their own ability to consent. Dr. Arielle Schwartz (2021) explains, "The fawn response involves people-pleasing to the degree that an individual disconnects from their own emotions, sensations, and needs."

> Fawn is a complicated trauma response because it looks like consent to those who are on the outside, but to the person experiencing it, they are in a state where their survival instinct has taken over.

Because of this, working with minors is a matter that requires careful consideration, planning and execution. Recently, when speaking about working with a minor, a director said to me, "This kid's a showbiz kid. She's used to the cussing and adult subject matter," as a point of good fortune and accessibility. As the minor's parents agreed to the material, this became a situation where offering the production team some questions to consider helped move them toward a more ethical framework. For example, asking production what rehearsals and shots the minor needs to be present for, when can a stand-in or double be used, and what are the non-negotiable shots the director needs in order to tell the story? Questions like these, coupled with thinking through the age and developmental stage of the child cast, and what was necessary for the child to be present, helped production shape a more consent-forward culture for this lone child actor in the midst of adult-centered emotional, heightened content. It often turns out that the minor does not need to be present for large sections of a scene, and a stand-in or double can alleviate exposure to content, as well as honor the working hours allowed.

In most cases, creating a balanced, supportive environment where minors can thrive can be done through preproduction with a qualified IC and a minors consultant, or one who is skilled in understanding the developmental psychology, actor's process and the nuances of the industry in order to help production make informed, ethical decisions. On occasion, an IC who specializes in working with minors may be necessary for a particularly complex situation, like scenes of emotional or physical abuse, non-consensual intimacy or scenes of extreme violence within the horror genre, for example. I often work as a consultant with ICs who find themselves in the midst of ongoing productions where scenes are added involving minors or minor actors are cast later. Issues may even arise on set where young adults need additional support, and understanding where they are developmentally can be helpful.

Preproduction

When working with minors as an IC, it is most important to know the child labor laws for the state where you will be working (kidcasting.com/child-labor-laws), any union regulations or guidelines, and how the production will be handling the moments of storytelling where heightened emotions and close relationships will be portrayed. Ideally, the production will bring in the IC as early as possible.

An effective IC will prove helpful in casting (if included in the process) by encouraging production to cast the oldest believable actor for the role, and help production and casting think through the callback process to ensure that the actor and their guardians are as fully informed as possible, and have had time to think about the project before accepting a role. The IC can also serve as a consultant in preproduction and ultimately help save time and money on set. Being able to negotiate expectations for the director and actors around the number of setups and takes for moments of intimacy or heightened emotional storytelling has proven effective in a variety of settings, and leaves everyone feeling positive knowing boundaries were honored and communication was clear. An effective IC will also help the guardians, production team, cast and crew prepare for set and remain ethical while shooting scenes of intimacy. Where ethics are concerned when working with minors, it means not only upholding the standards set by the profession, but also constantly considering any gaps that may exist in order to work toward creating an environment and experience that takes into consideration the wellbeing of the minor. For example, reminders to not joke with young performers in-between takes while filming a kiss scene can help mitigate insecurities and discomfort for everyone on set, so that the actors can focus on navigating the heightened emotions, close relationships and difficult moments common to screen-worthy storytelling.

On Set

Once on set, the lane for the IC remains the same as in production with adult performers. A qualified IC will mediate and problem shoot when necessary, but the IC's scope of practice remains concerned with supporting the performers and production in an ethical manner. All responsibility for the minor remains in the hands of the guardian in most cases. In California there is a relatively new position called the studio teacher/welfare worker whose job it is to ensure that production follows the law, and who also has the ability to pull a minor from set (https://www.dir.ca.gov/t8/11755.html). There has been an expressed interest by some who work with minors on sets who wonder how an IC might also be a studio teacher/welfare worker; however, this presents a problematic power dynamic between the minor and adult worker. The IC is there to work with the specific scene and does not interact with the child everyday. This ensures that the minor can separate those imaginary moments where they are playing heightened circumstances from their real, everyday life. This clear separation is ideal. Because the IC is rarely present every day of shooting and has a specific skillset to support moments of intimacy and heightened emotional storytelling, they will be able to maintain appropriate boundaries and represent the interests of the minor and their ability to fully consent without any vested interest beyond the ethical position they hold.

Our understanding of consent and its nuances in development are emerging and growing each year as science advances. We can still tell dynamic stories worthy of the screen with minors, but we can also do better in supporting these performers and their guardians so that they are able to consent to the best of their abilities with as much information as possible. We can use informed and thoughtful practices in preproduction to minimize the risk of harm and exercise professional boundaries that honor each individual and protect the most vulnerable among us. Through a thoughtful and consistent process, we can continue to do better for everyone involved, and while it may take more time in the preproduction, the outcomes often save time and money. It's also just the right thing to do.

Bibliography

Lai, Jennifer. "Old Enough to Vote, Old Enough to Smoke? Why are young people considered adults at age 18?" 23 April 2013. https://slate.com/news-and-politics/2013/04/new-york-minimum-smoking-age-why-are-young-people-considered-adults-at-18.html.

Maddaus, Gene. "*Romeo and Juliet* Stars Sue Paramount for Child Abuse Over Nude Scene in 1968 Film." 3 January 2023. https://variety.com/2023/film/news/romeo-and-juliet-child-abuse-nude-scene-lawsuit-1235477837/.

Rikard, Laura. "Consent in the Acting Classroom." *Theatrical Intimacy Education*. Asheville, January 2022. Workshop.

Schwartz, Arielle. *The Fawn Response in Complex PTSD*. 9 March 2021. https://drarielleschwartz.com/the-fawn-response-in-complex-ptsd-dr-arielle-schwartz/#.Y_kMhuzMJ6o.

The Annie E. Casey Foundation. "The Road to Adulthood: Aligning Child Welfare Practice with Adolescent Brain Development." 23 July 2017. https://www.aecf.org/resources/the-road-to-adulthood.

www.dir.ca.gov/t8/11755.html. n.d. February 2023.

www.dona.org. 28 January 2023.

A Conversation with Grace Byers

Brooke M. Haney

> Grace Byers plays Quinn on *Harlem*. The series hired an intimacy team, headed by Chelsea Pace. One of my favorites scenes I worked on was the first episode of season two, directed by Linda Mendoza, where Quinn had her first sexual experience with a woman, Isabella, played by Juani Feliz. Beyond simply talented, Grace is kind, generous, hilarious, incredibly skilled and takes notes like no actor I've worked with to this point. She's also the author of one of my favorite children's books, *I Am Enough*. So, I had to talk to her.

BROOKE   What advice would you give to early career actors who are working with an intimacy professional for their first time or working on a scene that might require an intimacy coordinator?

GRACE   Your body is a vessel that you are lending to the project. It does not belong to the project, it belongs to you. Therefore, you have the permission to use your voice in whatever way that you need to: vulnerably, respectfully, professionally, clearly, in order to ensure that you feel the safest in the most vulnerable of circumstances. It may be one of your first times speaking up and that can feel very difficult. That can feel a little out of place, like do I have the right to do it? You do. Because if you don't speak up and protect those parts of your being now, the aftermath is going to

	feel a whole lot more difficult to process than communicating your boundaries beforehand.
BROOKE	Why do you think it is hard to communicate beforehand?
GRACE	Apprehension is a big one. I know what this feels like. You don't want people to dislike you, get upset with you, think of you as a diva or, in the worst-case scenario, possibly get fired. It's important to continue to remind yourself: "my body is a vessel that I'm lending to the project, the project does not own my body." When you really know that truth deep down inside, it can give you the fortitude to be able to advocate for yourself and to know that, as you establish your own boundaries, it's going to feel awkward, it's going to feel clunky, you might not say everything perfectly at first, but to keep doing it because you're going to learn the language that you're going to need and, in the end, feel protected and taken care of.
BROOKE	Do you feel like you had any actual training around being able to articulate boundaries? Or do you feel like that's a thing you had to learn on the job?
GRACE	That's such a good question. Brooke, that's such a good question. For me, boundaries are a constant process of learning. That was a particular challenge for me personally, because I came from a people-pleasing background, which stemmed from my childhood. Being a CODA, a child of deaf adults, and being at the center of so much intersectionality, there was always a feeling of not being enough. A lot of children respond to that differently. For me, I didn't want to feel different, and not enough, so that turned into people pleasing.
BROOKE	What did that people pleasing look like?
GRACE	I tried to blend in as much as possible or not say anything that would: 1) make me stand out; 2) have people disagree with me; or 3) that could cause me to be criticized. I thought, let me just say all the "right things," do all the "right things," and this quickly turned into people pleasing. But, with that comes a denial of self and an eradication of boundaries. It wasn't until this last decade of my life, entering my thirties, that I realized that I was the one who was absorbing the hurt and the pain when I didn't speak up for myself.
	Sometimes establishing boundaries, and advocating for yourself, can feel isolating. But it's so important to stand in those boundaries, knowing that it is healthy, because you are your own

	individual who comes with your own individual experiences, and your boundaries are going to reflect that.
BROOKE	I know you're a person of faith.
GRACE	I am.
BROOKE	I grew up in a church, and I think, for some folks, pleasing people can come from their religion as well, and messages about selflessness. Has that affected you at all?
GRACE	I didn't find that. I understand the idea of selflessness around faith, but Jesus had boundaries. God has boundaries. And so I think that sometimes it's misinterpreted, that selflessness means that you are to abandon "self." And I don't think that that's the case. It's the idea of self fullness: I'm so full in my own self, that I'm able to then provide parts of myself to you, as opposed to abandoning myself entirely, and then just giving you the scraps of what I do have.
BROOKE	Thank you for sharing that. I love it. One thing I admired in your work, when we worked together on *Harlem*, was your skill at consistently finding the camera's frame. How did you hone that skill?
GRACE	When I started doing TV and film, years ago, *Empire* was my first TV/film gig, and I had never really known how to act within frame before. With stage work, it's the opposite. You take up the stage. There's positioning and blocking – both of which are much more expansive onstage. So that took me a while to learn for the camera, and a few cast members helped a lot.
BROOKE	How did the cast help you?
GRACE	There were times that they would physically adjust and say, "oh, I'm blocking your frame, or I'm blocking your light." I had to learn about proximity and positioning. I was so embarrassed because there were all of these phrases and terminologies being used, and I didn't know what many of them were. I remember asking Trai [Trai Byers is Grace's husband] in particular, "What does coverage mean?" It was sort of a training ground for me, as I learned so much about framing, lighting and some terminology.
BROOKE	What's one of the best pieces of advice you've been given about being on set?
GRACE	Befriend your camera crew. It's so important for you to be each other's allies and advocates. You both want the same thing: to secure an amazing shot. And when you work in cohesion with your camera crew, the work will reflect that. We love our crew on set for *Harlem*, they're really incredible. Our DP, Matt Edwards,

and the entire camera crew are amazing: not just wonderfully talented, but some of the kindest (and funniest) people you'll ever meet. We work in allyship constantly and often. I feel like the end product really reflects that.

BROOKE What kinds of questions do you ask?

GRACE What size is the frame? Can I move in this way and still be in frame? Often, I'll ask them to turn the monitor screen around so I'm able to see the impact of my movements in frame. I'll mark those perimeters in my mind. After that, I have the freedom to organically play. I'm not thinking about the frame, because I've already downloaded all of the information that I need. But that definitely took some time, it was a learning process.

BROOKE I'm glad you said the part about having them turn the monitor screen around, because that's one thing we did on *Harlem*. I always either brought the monitor to you or brought you to the monitor to see what the shot looked like. This is a thing I really like to do in intimate scenes, because it allows the actors to find the frame, and also to be able to see exactly what we are shooting so they know that it is within the boundaries of their rider.

GRACE Absolutely. It's less of an aesthetic thing, but it's more of: how can I maximize and optimize the scene in the best way, physically? If I'm turning my body in a certain way, and I realize, whenever I do that it either blocks the camera or it's not showing the full picture of what my body is going through, then that's always helpful for me.

BROOKE We had a conversation on set for *Harlem* about how the intimacy coordinator can support the actor around detailed storytelling. You, Juani, Linda and I spoke about how these two characters (Quinn and Isabella) had a very different level of experience around queer sex, and we decided to change the choreography a little bit to reflect that. What was that like for you?

GRACE I feel like you used such an important word here, choreography, because it's a dance. I think that an intimacy coordinator is not the first person that you would think of for "choreography" in that way. You might think, well, maybe the director will show me that or maybe that's something I'll work out with my scene partner or by myself. So it was very refreshing to be able to have an intimacy coordinator on set who could say, "hey, there's something that comes to my mind about this when it comes to Quinn's experience" and it can guide and lead the way in which we move in the scene together. To have been introduced to that added facet and tell that story through body language, with the help of an intimacy coordinator, was new for me, and very, very helpful in that process for Quinn.

BROOKE What other kinds of things can an intimacy coordinator do to help you do your best work?

GRACE It's added protection and safety if I have someone on set that can be my voice and help transcribe my boundaries. An intimacy coordinator, for me, has always been that person to liaise and liaise well, so that I don't ever have to be the person who's on set always fighting and saying no all the time to very personal things. It's really essential to be able to have someone listen to your comfort level boundaries and then regurgitate them back to me in a way that feels diplomatic and supportive. To also be able to relay these boundaries to the team. When you have that kind of support and security, ultimately it makes you feel like you can do your best work.

Intimacy and Disability   8

Brooke M. Haney

> I do not live with an apparent disability, however I do live with a few invisible disabilities including physical, neurological and psychological. Additionally, at the time of writing this chapter, I have worked for four and a half years as an actor with Only Make Believe, a theater company that goes into hospitals and schools for students with disabilities and does theatre with kids, many of whom have disabilities. My partner, Katie Blouse, who consulted on this chapter, has been a special education teacher in the New York City Department of Education for over ten years. Additionally, I surveyed folks with apparent physical disabilities in an online disability group I'm a part of about their thoughts on representation of disability in the media.

There are many conditions and disabilities, physical, mental and neurological, that are considered non-apparent. Selena Gomez has lupus, Millie Bobbie Brown lives with partial hearing loss, Orlando Bloom has dyslexia, Demi Lovato has bipolar disorder, Morgan Freeman and Lady Gaga both have fibromyalgia (a chronic pain condition), and Daniel Radcliffe lives with dyspraxia, a neurological condition that impairs movement and coordination.

We may not know before our actor intakes that someone in the cast has a disability. While we may give them the space to self disclose should they choose, disclosure should not be necessary in order for someone to request an accommodation. As I said in Part One, it is ethically imperative that intimacy professionals have competencies around non-apparent disability. The main focus of this chapter is to talk about the representation of apparent physical disabilities and the intimate storytelling around them.

No group is a monolith; different folks in the disability community prefer person-first or identity-first language. Some prefer non-apparent disability and find the language of invisible or hidden disability hurtful. Self-identification is a personal choice. For the purpose of this chapter, I will be alternating my language, however, it is important that when we work with actors we ask them which they prefer and honor that.

Storytelling

There is incredibly limited representation of disability in the media, and even less of intimacy and disability, so it is of heightened importance that, when we do work on these scenes, we do it respectfully and accurately, avoiding problematic tropes.

Some common, harmful tropes that we see in the storytelling around disability are:

Trauma tourism. Rooted in Rights, an organization that uses accessible digital media to advance the dignity, equality and self-determination of people with disabilities, writes that "[t]he trauma narrative focuses on stories such as dramatic life changing events. You'll often see stories in the media that focus on the 'tragic story' of disability…" This narrative exists to instill pity in the watcher.

Exploitive inspiration. Rooted in Rights also claims that "[w]hether it's the high school student asking a disabled person to prom, met with comments of 'aren't they incredible?' or videos of wheelchair users walking down the aisle at their wedding, this content is everywhere." This implies that overcoming a disability is the goal or a non-disabled person as savior should be celebrated.

Fetishization. Queer, disabled writer, Hannah Shewan Stevens writes:

> We all have our kinks, but there is a clear boundary between mutual fetish play and objectifying people without their consent. For disabled people, fetishization is a hidden assailant bubbling under the surface of society. 'Fetishization means seeing a disabled person as an object or a set of physical or intellectual characteristics that bring about sexual gratification,' explained Kaley Roosen, Ph.D., a clinical health

psychologist in Toronto. 'Instead of understanding a person as a whole, complicated individual, they are defined by their disability. So someone may fetishize a person's amputation or stump but fail to connect with the individual connected to that object of fetishization.'"

Media can be one of the greatest perpetrators of fetishization. While fetishes aren't wrong in and of themselves, when we create that as a dominant narrative for a particular group, the objectification goes outside the bounds of consensual kink and becomes harmful.

Breaking away from these tropes is imperative. When we do show intimacy and disability on stage or screen, we need to be cognizant of the gaze we are putting on the intimacy. Whose story are we centering? Be careful of assumptions you may have based on representation you've ingested. For example, do not assume that the character with the disability is the submissive one in the relationship. Each person is full of history, life experience, desires – vanilla or kinky, confidence and insecurities.

Preproduction

Director

My first stop is meeting with the director and getting aligned with their vision for the project and how the intimacy plays a part in telling the story. Depending on the ability and boundaries of the actor, some adjustments might need to be made to the director's initial ideas around the choreography, and there is also a lot you can do with the help of other departments.

Props and Scenic

Wedges can be purchased online or at your favorite sex store and are useful for finding or sustaining certain positions with ease for long periods of time. A yoga block can sometimes be used in a pinch. Your scenic team can adjust the height of the bed or the table to be just right. (Consider making this part of the storytelling if you are a writer.) Sliding chairs are fun, as are slings and swings. Look to some of the furniture in the kink world for inspiration on what may be both helpful in positioning and supportive of the story. Doing this far in advance is incredibly valuable so that, if something needs to be purchased, customized or refigured, you aren't holding up production on a day of filming.

Consultants

Work with a consultant who has expertise on the specific disability. They can advise on how the disability affects the character's movement, flexibility, balance and other things that might impact how they have sex. Talk with them to make sure you understand how and where that character would experience sensation, both sexually and if any movements or positions might cause pain. Use what you learn to create realistic choreography that you can present to the director and actor.

Actor Intake Meetings

Just like you would ask an actor about which pronouns they use, ask an actor with a disability if they prefer person-first or identity-first language. Set up respectful communication in order to prevent hurt. You may need to educate the other actors in the scene or other collaborators around some of this etiquette.

When you are talking about boundaries, be sure to ask about any assistive devices like walkers, canes or wheelchairs. These are extensions of the person's body and should be treated with that respect. It would be inappropriate to sit on someone's lap without consent; leaning on someone's chair without permission is also wrong. However, choreographing taboos in an interesting and compelling way could be an option if it is intentional and works with the actor's boundaries.

Ask questions about what kinds of support they need not only around their boundaries, but around executing the choreography as well. Do they have any communication, navigation, flexibility, strength, mobility or endurance concerns? Giving lots of information about what to expect as well as what accommodations are already available will give actors an idea of the kinds of support they can ask for. Asking about their learning style (i.e. visual, auditory, kinesthetic, reading, writing) will give you information on how to best teach the choreography and give notes. For example, while we don't demonstrate choreography on actors, for a visual learner having a second IC or assistant IC on set to show the choreography might be quite helpful.

Choreography Considerations

If you are working on a scene with a character with a disability, it is important to know how the disability affects the way the character experiences sensation and pleasure. Remember that people who use wheelchairs may do so for a range of reasons. This means that many people can still have full sensation and control of their genitals – including those with spinal cord injuries (SCI). However, for some people, their disability can impact sexual function such as a loss or change in sensation, difficulty controlling the muscles, and some penis owners may not be able to achieve or maintain an erection. Even so, some people who don't have feeling below the waist experience great pleasure from stimulation in areas like the arms, earlobe, neck, cheek and nipple – so much so that it can even lead to orgasm.

If the choreography has been prescribed by the script or the director and doesn't work for the actors' bodies, you may need to make adjustments. As you make adjustments, your impulse may be to start from the baseline, trying to change as little as possible. However, I encourage you to step further back and consider all the possibilities. Limitations are often the catalyst for fantastic, creative storytelling.

> A series that has done some good work around intimacy and disability is *Special* on Netflix, starring actor-writer Ryan O'Connell. Another scene that shows some wonderful nuance is the scene between Micah (Leo Sheng) and Maribel (Jillian Mercado) in *The L Word: Generation Q* in season two episode five.

When the script is vague, i.e. "they kiss" or "they have passionate sex," start with the director's vision around how the intimacy impacts the arc of the story and the relationship of these characters. Knowing the point of the scene is sometimes more informative than simply an initial idea for staging. Consider your definition of sex. Most of the media perpetuates a very able bodied, thin, cis, straight and white idea of what sex is, in which a man and woman have vaginal intercourse until one or both of them climax. However, sex is simply how any one person, couple or group of partners define it.

The brain is often considered the largest and most effective sex organ. Stimulating it, whether with fantasies, dirty talk or innuendo is a huge turn on. Look in the text for opportunities for obvious, subtextual or double entendre. Perhaps the character's body relaxes (or tenses) in response. What happens with their breath?

Arguably any part of the body can be an erogenous zone; quite frankly, an official count is hard to come by. That said, some of the non-genital erogenous zones that can be useful to consider when building choreography are: scalp, ears, neck, lips, chest/breast/nipples/pecs, navel, lower stomach, arm pits, inner arms, wrists, hands, sacrum, inner thighs, behind the knees, feet and toes. If you take these parts of the body and layer on the ingredients of choreography, some pretty incredible and detailed moments of intimacy are possible. Use strength and tempo of the action to create the level of passion. Gaze and destination can show desire and intent. Add response, secondary action and the breath, always the breath! Chelsea Pace details a list of ingredients for choreographing intimacy in *Staging Sex*. Sometimes I enjoy working with Laban or Viewpoints as well.

Final Thoughts

In general, when working on a scene that involves intimacy and a character or characters with disabilities, having folks on the creative team with lived experience of those disabilities is invaluable. Listen to them and, if you do not have personal experience with the same disability as the story, be careful not to let your lens override theirs. In these cases, our job is to help translate their vision to the stage or screen. A note to directors and producers: a significant number of disabled people I interviewed said, without prompting, that they feel strongly that we must end Hollywood's obsession with crip-face. All disabled characters should be played by disabled actors. That said, remember that we never ask an actor about their personal intimate experiences. Their job is to act, not to educate us on how folks with disabilities have sex. If there aren't already disabled creatives on the team, bringing in a consultant is a way to ensure that the representation of the intimacy is not only respectful, but accurate and realistic.

Resources

Demystifying Disability: What to Know, What to Say, and How to be an Ally
This book, written by disabilities rights activist Emily Landau who is the editor in chief of the *Rooted in Rights* blog (also a great resource), is approachable and written to be empowering. It covers some history, how to talk (and ask) about disability, representation in the media and more. It is straightforward, welcoming and galvanizing.

Sins Invalid: An Unshamed Claim to Beauty

This 32-minute documentary highlights years of work by Sins Invalid whose live performances explore themes of sexuality and disability while centering the experiences of queer, gender-variant and artists of color.

Skin, Tooth, and Bone: The Basis of Movement is Our People

A galvanizing Disability Justice Primer, based on the work of Patty Berne and Sins Invalid. It contains history and context as well as specific ideas around mixability organizing and access suggestions for events. I recommend the second edition as it has several additional resources.

Bibliography

Louise, Shona. "Disability Is More than Just Inspiration or Trauma. When Will Media Cover It Authentically?" *Rooted in Rights*, 27 July 2021, rootedinrights.org/disability-is-more-than-just-inspiration-or-trauma-when-will-media-cover-it-authentically/.

Stevens, Hannah Shewan. "Is Disabled Fetishization a Harmless Kink or Destructive Objectification?" *Giddy*, 6 May 2022, getmegiddy.com/disabled-fetishization.

A Conversation with Ryan J. Haddad

Brooke M. Haney

> Ryan J. Haddad is a disabled writer, actor and autobiographical performer with cerebral palsy, known for his recurring role in Netflix's *The Politician*. Despite having toured his solo play *Hi, Are You Single?* for seven years, when it came time for a two-week sit down at Woolly Mammoth Theatre Co, artistic director Maria Manuela Goyanea suggested that Ryan and his director, Laura Savia, engage with intimacy choreographer Chelsea Pace to prepare. In this interview, I talk with Ryan about his work with Chelsea as well as his mission to use his work to sexualize disabled bodies.

BROOKE   How did you react when Laura told you Woolly Mammoth wanted you to bring in an intimacy coordinator?

RYAN   I just balked at it for a moment. Not that I don't think there's value in intimacy coordinators, but I had always known them to exist when it was a scene between two individuals or more. And so the idea of a solo play, in which I'm playing myself, I was like, to whom is there to be intimate?

BROOKE   So what happened?

RYAN   I realized that it's about emotional intimacy and that that can also mean with yourself. Chelsea sort of made me sit with the text and acknowledge that it is a performance, but it's also not the

	easiest material to take on every night. And it was a sort of, "No, let's sit with you now as a 30-year-old adult who wrote this when you were 23 and talk about the emotional implications of what is on the page and what you've tasked yourself with."
BROOKE	Was that helpful?
RYAN	I think it was, because frankly it was the longest I had ever performed any of my work in sequence. And as I matured as a human I needed to mature as a performer, which meant landing in the same emotional places, repeatedly.
BROOKE	Did you work with Chelsea on any choreography?
RYAN	That is what I would say was the most helpful. The choreography was really riveting and illuminating and she did help me find intimacy with myself. What happens in the script is, "We open on Ryan with his shorts at his ankles massaging his underwear, talking to a man on FaceTime to try to get off." But by the end of the first page, he has sort of stopped. Like the sexy questions that the man asks, who you don't hear or see, take him out of the moment and make him do this kind of quirky, comedic, vulnerable confessional, while some other guy is literally on FaceTime doing this (stroking gestures) and not listening or paying attention. And so a lot of what I always used to do – it was a choose your own adventure.

Where do I want to sit up? Where do I want to lean forward? Do I want to turn the phone here or there? But once the sort of sexiness breaks, I never went back to it or activated my sensuality in any way. |
BROOKE	What changed with the choreography?
RYAN	So what Chelsea did, with my director in collaboration, was keep the sexuality of the moment alive so that we weren't going for the comedic gimmick, or we weren't going for the tenderness of the more poignant elements. To start it was the masturbation. Then I would stop that, but I would still be sitting there with a bare chest and a bare stomach.
BROOKE	What did you add?
RYAN	It was a lot of touching of the chest and choosing moments to sort of circle my nipples. And I wore a gold chain that has one of my late aunt's crosses. And I twirled that as I was having this intimate sexual moment. That's fascinating as well to sort of activate the Christianity of childhood. And then I would play with my ear a little bit and come back to my chest. It took a moment of 30 seconds and turned it into a moment with my heart and my

	whole body for four minutes. Also it created consistency in the performance, which I hadn't had before.
BROOKE	Had you tried other ways of trying to be consistent before?
RYAN	Without the intimacy coordinator, there was a lot of lean forward, lean back, to the side, to the side. It was about blocking more than it was about intimacy. And I remember sometimes being frustrated. Shifting my body positions had just never felt like enough. But I didn't know enough to realize that intimacy choreography was what I was craving.
BROOKE	How was the intimacy choreography different from simply blocking?
RYAN	By tying it to certain parts of my body and making it not just gesture, but connection with myself, I understood it as an actor, and I understood what it meant for the character and why there was value in it. Even though, at the beginning, I didn't understand what value an intimacy coordinator could bring to a solo masturbation scene, where I wasn't actually masturbating, I realized that the small details were really powerful and changed the way I played the scene from an emotional standpoint. Then I was very happy with it.
BROOKE	Can you talk to me a little bit about representation of disability and intimacy on TV/film?
RYAN	Yeah, prior to the last three or five years, it was very much this disabled character played by a non-disabled actor is going to be seen in the beginnings of a sex scene and then we're gonna cut away. That sort of media is powerful and disabled people have been so excluded from narratives for so long that we have a lot of catching up to do in changing perceptions.
BROOKE	You've been vocal that disabled characters should be played by disabled actors. In *Demystifying Disability* you say that besides simply being the right thing to do, non-disabled actors need to learn to move like someone with a disability and then layer on the acting, but a disabled actor needs only to act. Do you think that every disabled actor should only play a role with exactly their same experience?
RYAN	This is a complicated question and I think there's nuance to it, and I also think my own ideas about it continue to evolve. This question is very big and could encompass neurodiversity, cognitive/intellectual disabilities, sensory disabilities, or a whole host of invisible disabilities that cannot be outwardly identified. I only

feel comfortable speaking from my experience as someone with a mobility disability.

There's an argument to be made that characters in wheelchairs should be played by actors who use wheelchairs. I'm not quadriplegic or paraplegic, but given efforts to cast disabled actors in disabled roles, those character breakdowns still arrive in my inbox sometimes. And then I have to read the role and ask myself, "Should I be playing this? Do I have a connection to this character?" Those experiences feel very different from mine, and I haven't played one of those roles yet, but I'm not saying I never would. I think it depends on the story. And I don't think the answer to this question should be reduced entirely to diagnosis or someone's personal mobility device.

BROOKE Can you give me an example?

RYAN Well, there's a huge push among disability advocates to expand job opportunities for disabled talent. We want to be considered for many roles, not only the ones where the character has a disability. But in terms of playing a disabled character, I don't think I should have to count myself out if the character doesn't specifically have cerebral palsy. There are lots of people with adjacent mobility disabilities whose experiences are similar to mine, sometimes even more so than another person with cerebral palsy because cerebral palsy itself encompasses a huge spectrum.

And in terms of a specific mobility device, I don't see a lot of people, especially adults, walking around with the kind of walker I've used since I was three years old. So not many roles are written with my specific mobility device in mind. But I know many, many people who are ambulatory wheelchair users, which is to say their chosen mobility device is a wheelchair, but they can also walk in certain circumstances of their choice. Just in the way that my chosen mobility device is a walker, but I can walk independently in certain environments depending on my comfort level. And so there are people with my degree of cerebral palsy, or my similar manifestation of cerebral palsy, whose primary way of getting around is a chair or scooter. And yes, I absolutely think I can play those roles, if the experience of the character is close to mine. Because at that point it becomes about what mobility device this character has chosen, what mobility device makes them most comfortable? And as I age as a human, not an actor, there's no telling what mobility device I might end up using later in life.

One other component of this is, there are people with cerebral palsy, or MS, or who are amputees, who don't use mobility devices at all in their daily life, or at least at certain points in time. Their needs are dynamic and can change, ebb and flow. And so should they not also be considered for roles that match their disability or experience simply because they're currently able to move without a cane or crutches or walker or wheelchair? That feels very sticky to me! I've never moved through the world publicly without my walker, so I don't have that experience. But I imagine it enters the territory of telling someone with cerebral palsy or MS or another kind of physical disability that they're not "disabled enough," they don't present "disabled enough" for a certain role, and that doesn't feel good to me either. If you can find the exact right performer to convey the exact type of mobility disability that's on the page, fantastic. But maybe you can also adapt what you envisioned on the page to fit the actor you want to cast. I don't think we've reached a time yet where we should close doors that have only recently started to open.

BROOKE   In *Dark Disabled Stories* you write a lot about intimacy. When you write, it seems like intimacy is integral to your work.

RYAN   Absolutely. It's political, frankly. My mission, for this first chapter of my career, but probably going forward, has been sexualizing disabled bodies. I'm a storyteller in the first person, so that more specifically means my disabled body. The world doesn't see us as objects of romance or desire or affection; that's why I have trouble dating. I mean, it feels like that's reducing it, but I think that when I walk into a gay space and I'm feeling hot and feeling like I'd like to make a connection, I'm sort of categorically denied those connections. No one sees a disabled person with a mobility device as a choice or an option for them, rarely do they. (There are lots of disabled people in relationships with those who are not disabled. I haven't had that luck, as it were.)

And because of this, I think that the more I show myself being sexy and the more I show the character of Ryan in sexual situations, the more an audience and the public at large, depending on how wide the audience for my work becomes, will start to see disabled people differently.

BROOKE   Media is super powerful in that way.

Working with Fat Actors 9

*Katherine Blouse and
Brooke M. Haney*

> We are a straight-sized, white, non-binary intimacy coordinator and a fat white woman writing this chapter. We acknowledge our lack of superfat and infinifat experience as well as our lens as white folks talking about an issue steeped in racism and how this limits our writing. Working with actors of all sizes should be a competency in this industry, but considering the extremely limited representation of fat folks portraying simulated sex on TV and in film, we are including it here as a specialty in hopes that this chapter will help it to become a competency.

Due to the extreme fatphobia in our culture, perpetuated by the media, fatness is perhaps the only identity where it is still socially acceptable to use a negative connotation as a slur. In her book *The Body is Not an Apology*, Sonya Renee Taylor says:

> We learned the language of fatphobia and weight stigma, the language of difference shaming. We were becoming fluent in body terrorism, either as perpetrators or as inactive bystanders, not because we were bad people but because we were in an immersion school of body shame.

TV and film has been one of the perpetrators, part of the school of body shame. A disproportionately high percentage of characters on TV and in film and theatre are thin (and white). If you look at the statistics around the percentage of the population that wears plus size clothing in America, without any other intersections, we are leaving out over half the population from our storytelling. The lack of representation becomes even more dire when we think about leading and romantic roles. Fat actors are often relegated to the sassy best friend or shy loner, characters void of sexuality.

Language

Definitions

You may notice we're using the word fat. We suggest you do too. While it is socially charged and has been weaponized, it isn't inherently bad. The word "fat" is a neutral descriptor of size, and when we avoid it we are assigning negative value to being fat. Everything exists on a spectrum, and this includes fatness. When people talk about the fat privilege spectrum, they are most often referring to how folks self-describe their fatness. Charlotte Zoller, in her column *Ask a Fat Girl*, explains that words like mid size, small fat, med fat, large fat, superfat, infinifat and death fat are "a set of terms created by and for the fat community to self-identify one's size." This framework was first coined by Ash, of *The Fat Lip Podcast*. The larger someone is, the more discrimination they face and the harder it is to access clothing, affirming healthcare, travel, public spaces, etc. While there is some positive representation of smaller fats in media, that representation becomes scarce to non-existent as you move along the spectrum.

Helpful and harmful language

There are plenty of synonyms and genteelisms for fat, some with and some without inherent judgment. Using descriptive words isn't necessarily wrong; how we use them makes a difference. I (Brooke) once worked with a director, who in a notes session described a fat actress's movement as matronly. The actress was playing a 14-year-old having sex for her first time. Matronly was intentionally used to insult. It did nothing to communicate an effective note. This kind of passive euphemism, dripping in fatphobia, is insidious.

As choreographers, we know to desexualize language and we have words to communicate changes around choreography that aren't loaded. Rather than a descriptive euphemism, we might suggest a change in tempo, duration or gravity.

Harmful Tropes

The "body terrorism" that Taylor talks about above is amplified by the harmful tropes we perpetuate on TV and in film. This is not an exhaustive list, but some of the most common ones to lookout for are:

- The fetishizing or desexualizing of fat Black women. For a historical example of fetishization, look to the story of Saartjie Baartman, who was put on display, semi-nude, all over Europe in the nineteenth century. Suzan Lori Parks's play *Venus* is a thoughtful depiction of this story. The mammie trope, an example of desexualization, is based on the history where "enslaved, maternal black women were desexualized, their bodies used for the reproductive needs of white women and to care for their babies" (Haney, 2023).
- Oblivious fat men who have very "hot" wives or girlfriends and it befuddles – think Jerry Gergich on *Parks and Recreation*. This type of comedy relies on the idea that it is ridiculous for a fat person to find love and lust, especially with someone who isn't also fat.
- Similarly the trope where a thin, conventionally attractive person "sees beyond" someone's fatness, falling in love with them despite it, and is therefore inspiring in their exceptional goodness.
- The savior trope; when the football player takes the fat girl who has been bullied to prom, saving her from bullies, reinforces the idea that fatness is something to pity or that having sex with someone who is fat is doing them a favor.
- Fat men die of heart attacks during sex in the media far too often, reinforcing the fallacy that a fat person is automatically unhealthy.
- The thin character who used to be fat, most often portrayed by a thin actor in a fat suit – think Monica in *Friends*, Terry in *Brooklyn Nine-Nine*.

While the intimacy coordinator doesn't have a say in casting and thus doesn't make decisions around what actors will end up being in a scene that involves fat sex, it felt important to us to still include this. Do. Not. Use. Fat. Suits. There are plenty of talented fat actors and putting thin actors in fat suits not only restricts the work of fat actors, it is also an inaccurate, harmful portrayal of fatness.

Other Considerations

In working with fat actors and storylines dealing with fat culture, what follows are some necessary areas of cultural competency. As with other identities, if you are not fat, consider hiring a consultant who can advise you.

Racism and Religion

It is important to understand where our biases are rooted. In *Fearing the Black Body*, Sabrina Strings explains:

> [T]wo critical historical developments contributed to a fetish for svelteness and a phobia about fatness: the rise of the transatlantic slave trade and the spread of Protestantism. Racial scientific rhetoric about slavery linked fatness to "greedy" Africans. And religious discourse suggested that overeating was ungodly.

This is a simplification necessary here and we encourage you to read Strings's book. Just as we are a society steeped in white supremacy in America, our internalized fatphobia goes deep. As a result, microaggressions around fatness run rampant in our culture and may occur on set. It is important for us to recognize this history and look to the fat liberation movement for a reeducation.

Medical Bias

If working on a medical scene with a fat person, be aware that it wasn't until recently that being fat was considered unhealthy. The change in the medical field wasn't due to innovative research, but to racism and the desire for white women to look less like Black women. Look to the Health at Every Size movement for guidelines on how to represent affirming health care.

Queer Culture

While gay male culture can be an incredibly fatphobic community, subcultures within it can be affirming. Chubs and larger Bears are consensually celebrated and sexualized specifically for their size. Despite the lack of size diversity on shows like *The L Word*, the lesbian community has distance from patriarchy and the male gaze, resulting in a greater amount of fat positivity.

Kink

There are, in the kink community, fatness related fetishizes. There are folks who seek crushing or suffocation as part of their sexual play as well as folks who identify as chasers, gainers, feeders, feedees and encouragers. Any presentation of this should be done with someone with a kink competency or specialization so as to avoid misrepresentation. Additionally, while fetishizing can be fun in reciprocal, consent-based relationships, storytelling that gives permission to fetishize or objectify a group without consent is harmful. Be mindful.

Coordinating with Departments

If the script is specifically talking about the character's weight as bad or unhealthy, the actor is personally experiencing microaggressions or direct discrimination by the writing. Be aware of this and work with the director and AD, the wardrobe and crew for a set that operates within fat liberation.

Regardless of the size of the actor, do not comment on the actor's body positively or negatively. When it is necessary to choose language to talk about a fat person's body, always defer to the words that person likes to use, whether it is fat, plus size, curvy or something else.

Think about the width of the actor's chair while they are waiting; for example, a traditional "director's chair" might not have enough space between the armrests for an actor to sit comfortably. Beyond comfort, the armrests may leave marks on the actor's thighs that you don't want on camera.

Remind wardrobe to have properly sized modesty robes; make sure that modesty garments and barriers are large enough for the actor's body. Several companies that make modesty garments either make them larger (though even the larger ones aren't that big) so that they can be trimmed to fit, or do not charge extra for special ordering a custom size. However, you must plan in advance if you need the time for something made to order.

Awareness of the furniture on set is important. Unless the story is specifically addressing lack of accessibility, the furniture should be large enough for the actors. Talk with the set dresser and props team about heights, widths and the weight capacity of anything being used for simulated sex or other intimacy.

Choreographic Considerations

Fat people aren't always self-conscious, nervous or uncomfortable being naked or having sex. Writers, don't put your fatphobia onto your characters. ICs, don't assume the actor's relationship to their body. In your actor intake meetings, give opportunities for boundary setting as you always do, but don't be precious about it.

Finding positions that work for the actors' bodies might necessitate a little experimentation. Lots of companies make wedges, ramps, lifts and other assistive positioning pillows. Liberator's products come in a variety of shapes and sizes up to 42" in width. *Big Big Love,* by Hanne Blank, is an excellent resource and has a chapter on "Titillation and Tactics: Practical Sex for People of All Sizes." It not only details position accommodations, but also ways to adapt toys for all bodies.

While actual sex in the water can be difficult due to lack of lubrication, water as a supportive element is fantastic, including for positions that might not be possible otherwise. So, simulated sex in a hot tub, swimming pool or jacuzzi would make for excellent steamy storytelling.

Positive Examples

While they can be difficult to find, there are some positive examples of fat sexuality. We include some here so you have a starting place for research, inspiration or to share with a creative team who is trying to make their storytelling more fat positive.

All of *Shrill*. Seriously. Aidy Bryant's character has a full, fun, sexy, slutty life. In particular, check out the scene in season 1 episode 5.

Gabourey Sidibe and Mo McRae's rooftop sex scene in *Empire* season two episode six. It's also worth looking at the negative and hateful responses to that scene, to know what your actors may be up against.

On Broadway, Tony Winner Bonnie Milligan as Princess Penelope, the most beautiful woman in the kingdom, in *Head over Heels* was not just a gorgeous representation of fat romance, but of queerness as well.

In *Magic Mike XXL*, there is a scene in a members only club where a stripper, played by Michael Strahan, picks up a fat woman he is dancing for. Not only does this scene actively work against a lot of fatphobic stereotypes, it is also an example of interesting use of furniture.

Bibliography

Blank, Hanne. *Big Big Love: A Sourcebook on Sex For People of Size*, Greenery Press, 2000.
Haney, Brooke M. "A Conversation with Felichia Chivaughn." 26 August 2023.
String, Sabrina. *Fearing the Black Body: The Racial Origins of Fat Phobia*, New York University Press, 2019.
Taylor, Sonya Renee. *The Body is Not an Apology: The Power of Radical Self-Love*, Brett-Koehler Publishers, Inc., 2018.
Zoller, Charlotte. "What Terms Like 'Superfat' and 'Small Fat' Mean, and How They Are Used." *TeenVogue*, 6 April 2021, https://www.teenvogue.com/story/superfat-small-fat-how-they-are-used.

A Conversation with Jen Ponton

Brooke M. Haney

> Jen Ponton is a hilarious and nuanced fat actress with a decades long career. She is perhaps best known for her role as Rubi in *Dietland* and as champion of fat liberation. In 2020, she did her first TEDx talk on "Hollywood's Fat Phobia Problem" and has spoken widely on what it means to be a fat actor in romantic scenes in Hollywood. At the time of our conversation, Jen was working with intimacy coordinator Alison Novelli, and amidst the beginning of production graciously agreed to talk with me.

BROOKE   Why is it so important for us to see fat folks having simulated sex on TV and in film?

JEN   What's very specific about marginalized people is that they are often desexed without their permission. Certain marginalized communities, like Asian or AAPI men, find that they're very desexed, and Asian or AAPI women are hypersexualized, in very specific ways. But with fat folks, especially white fat folks, we are totally desexed. The stories that are laid out for fat white characters almost never include romance and sexuality. My ethos is that when we see something, we can be it. That helps inform what we think we deserve in our real lives. It's a permission slip that we shouldn't have to need.

BROOKE	Has this been true for you?
JEN	I really believe that of the things that I now know that I'm capable of doing and that I deserve in the world, it's because I saw it happen to a marginalized character first. It's not because I lived in a fatphobic, night terror of a society and was like, "oh, I deserve love and care and respect and desire in my life." It's because I read about it in books. It's because I saw all of these other underdog characters inhabiting it and thought that maybe it could one day be transferred to me. The more we see those marginalized voices living full lives and we are connecting with them and their vulnerability, the more we soften toward them. So that's where I think, for fat characters in particular, sexuality and success are very important, because we see it so often portrayed as loneliness and failure.
BROOKE	Your first simulated sex scene was in *Love on the Run*, right?
JEN	We filmed in 2011 and it came out in 2016 and there were no intimacy coordinators in the whole landscape, but our team was very professional and we had a closed set.
BROOKE	How was it choreographed?
JEN	I think the two actors just had to figure out what to do. I believe that our director, the late Ash Christian, gave us the overarching gist of what he wanted to see. And he was like, "you know, it's not very long. There's a little pleasure, make sure you do this, and you know, just go ahead." My scene partner Steve Howey was coming from *Shameless* where he had done a ton of intimacy work, so he was not fazed, but he is also standard industry "hot." I was feeling so green. I remember I was like "do I just have to be myself in this moment?" The fact that there was just no guidance, no protection, no hand to hold, felt like it could edge toward exploitative.
BROOKE	Thanks for sharing that. We should never ask our actors to bring their personal lives from their own bedrooms to set. You're working on a film right now with an intimacy coordinator, right? Who is it?
JEN	The amazing Alison Novelli.
BROOKE	How is working with an intimacy coordinator different?
JEN	Oh my God. Everything. I feel like I have an advocate. I feel like there's a gentle hand on my back and I feel a ton of consent and safety in the blocking. Alison is like the personification of a gut feeling – always reminding me to drop in, breathe, regulate my

body. Even outside of intimacy, in more stunt-like moments where I have a lot of fear and adrenaline going on. The warm up games are so helpful, and the guidance through boundaries, and that these boundaries are totally okay. But it's because we're voicing them, right? Just like any good therapist would say, I think it's only really a boundary if you put it out there.

BROOKE How is the simulated sex in this movie different from *Love on the Run*?

JEN This film is going to be different from *Love on the Run* because, in fact, my pleasure is a huge part of it, which is fabulous. In *Love on the Run*, sex in the scene is really just a diversion that leads to a death, versus this character being given an orgasm caught on camera as a major plot point, as a major arc. There's a camera on my face as I receive pleasure and that's huge, that's amazing and I have so appreciated Alison really making a safe container for that, where I could live the character to her fullest, but not feel like a piece of meat. Like my co-star will be fine hiding behind my thigh, right? I'm the one who has the camera right on my mug and I have to sell it with breath and with sounds that I choose and with dynamics, making a symphony of my own design. So, just the protection and the comfort that that gives me not needing to feel exploited and bare and like if I want to show up on the day and do something really really really vulnerable just for me I can do it. If I want to do something that I have crafted like a piece of music, I can do that too.

BROOKE Was there anything that surprised you?

JEN In their initial talks with me, Alison was like, "we can avoid intimacy on whatever dates you have your menstrual cycle." And I was like, "We can, what? This is amazing. That makes a difference for me." Feeling like I have someone there whose primary function is to make sure that I feel cared for enough that I can show up in my best artistry.

BROOKE Yes! Is there advice you would give to other fat actors who are doing their first scene of intimacy?

JEN Advocate for yourself and make sure that the people who are working with you so closely – not your scene partners, but your intimacy coordinator and your wardrobe designer – really understand your body. I feel very lucky and grateful because in this production where I am a fat body and those two individuals are straight-sized people (Lawrence Guilliard Jr. and Patch Darragh), they've been so cognizant and thoughtful and deliberate with me. Like the tiny neoprene modesty garments are inappropriately small. They were so mindful with me about how these can be really limited in what they cover. They said "try it on, see how it feels and we can custom make you a garment."

Do not be afraid to speak up, because most people do want you to feel respected and safe and dignified in your body. I'm sure some people are assholes, but I think in general most people want you to feel embodied and that you raising any concerns is only going to help them do their jobs better and help you deliver on the day.

I would also say, be willing to bring up any movement questions or any simulation questions to the intimacy coordinator. If you're concerned about your partner, if you're concerned about how your body will be portrayed in a certain position, these people are your advocates. They will help you find positions that you feel comfortable in, that don't have you shying away from the camera. They'll help you find something that's honest, real, moving and that you're comfortable with.

BROOKE Do you have advice for intimacy coordinators who are working with fat actors?

JEN I would say that if an intimacy coordinator is concerned that they're not serving fat actors to the best of their capability, one of the best things you can do is become accustomed to the way a fat body really moves. Again, because of so much media denial and erasure, if you're not a fat person and you're not hanging out with a lot of fat folks and you're not having intimate relationships with fat folks, you might not know.

And I think that's really key, and not just in sexual circumstances, but like out dancing or fat strippers. Right? If intimacy coordinators want to bone up on fat bodies, seek out fat expressions of pleasure. Even in queer pornography, like where there's great representation and just capturing that pleasure and watching what's effective and evocative on camera. I can't believe I'm recommending porn but companies like Aorta films, right?

BROOKE Aorta creates wonderful work.

JEN What a gorgeous blend of cinematography and porn, and the picture of these other bodies and their pleasure and their divinity is so well captured. And when you can find that it's very powerful and then you can sort of add that to your mental rolodex.

	The ways that fat bodies essentially move are just inherently different, not necessarily from straight-sized people, but definitely from like very willowy people.
BROOKE	Do you have an example?
JEN	One of the first intimacy scenes that I'm going to have in this film, *Resentment*, is a strip tease on top of a bar, very *Coyote Ugly*. It's gonna be really fun. The person that they first took on who was lovely, was thin like a swizzle stick, and she was choreographing things for me with her very, very long arms, they went on forever. Because she was so slender too, they could wrap all the way around her body. I can barely get my arms around my chest. Right? And so the things that she was doing to convey her own sensuality just didn't translate, but that doesn't mean that I don't have my own.
BROOKE	Any last thoughts?
JEN	If you're dealing with fat actors in intimacy, remember that their world experience has been very gaslighting, very antagonistic. We all have to get to a certain point of okay-ness with it, or pushing against it, to even become actors in the first place, but all of us are still that same seventh-grader on the inside to a non-trivial extent. Just coming from that level of empathy, and awareness, so that you always know exactly how to come back to an actor. Make it about their confidence in the moment and telling this story. Bring it back to the power they hold, and you'll get to tell stories that are revolutionary for our bodies and for the world.

10

Black American Intimacy
Considerations for Choreography and Practice

Kaja Dunn

> Kaja Dunn was the first person to offer classes on race and intimacy choreography. She works as an intimacy professional on TV/film and in theatre on Broadway, regionally and in academia. She is the Equity, Diversity and Inclusion affiliate faculty for Theatrical Intimacy Education as well as an associate professor at the Carnegie Mellon School of Drama. Because of her vast experience as well as expertise, I asked her to write a chapter on Black American intimacy to upcoming IPs looking to specialize in that area. My hope is that by being specific, folks looking to specialize in other types of racialized stories can translate her wisdom onto their specialty as well.

Race and Culture in Intimacy Work

Race and culture are of critical importance when doing intimacy choreography. The work of an intimacy professional is sometimes compared to that of a fight choreographer, and while often there's overlap with people doing both things, there are key and critical differences. Intimacy practices, sex, sexuality and sexual tropes have also been used by colonist forces to shape tropes and stereotypes about people in the global majority.

I specialize in culturally competent choreography. White colonizers used sex and sexual tropes as tools to dehumanize and justify the exploitation, degradation, abuse, torture, rape and assault of colonized peoples. They developed tropes that still persist in contemporary culture and media. We aren't starting with a blank slate. Centuries of sexualized tropes of Black women and men have been fed into the consciousness and psyche of Americans and people around the world. "Cultural studies scholars have devoted considerable attention to studies of media audiences, institutions, technologies, and texts" (Brooks and Herbert, 2006, p. 297). Black women are the foundation of this vein of cultural studies, which looks at the intersections of race and gender representation in the media. Until about two decades ago, the bulk of contemporary research in this area in the United States focused on Black women: "Many of the arguments made previously about Black women also apply to women from India, Latin America, Puerto Rico, and Asia, "albeit through the historical specificity of their distinctive group histories" (Hill Collins, 2004, p. 12).

When it comes to the subject of Black American love and intimacy and larger intimacy practice in general, foremothers bell hooks, Audre Lorde, Toni Morrison, Tarana Burke, Angela Davis and many others have laid the groundwork for the field long before the field of intimacy work had begun.

In addition to content of a sexual nature, intimacy may also include content that encompasses identity, things like race, disability, religion, age or other heightened personal experiences with appropriate cultural context and competency.[1] These are acts of intimacy that exist in a deeply cultural context. At the heart of it, the negotiations we engage in as Black people who must navigate both our own multiple histories and the complexity of the "outside gaze" means that to choreograph our bodies in both intra- and interracial scenes takes nuance and an understanding of theory and history.

The Specificity of Black American Intimacy Work

This chapter will speak to Black Americans: their specificity, resilience, the ways in which intimacy shows up in all orientations. One can think of the diversity of Black love the same way they think about the diversity of Black music: we have jazz, trap, rap, hip-hop, soul, R&B, gospel music. When thinking about Black intimacy in performance, one has to think of what lies just below the surface. To perform Black intimacy is to incorporate the joy, resilience, trauma, strength and story of the Black body.

A quick note about language here; racial language is intentionally fluid. For the purposes of this chapter, when I use the term "Black," I am referring to Black Americans, and use this when referring to intimacy as a people and identity. This framing may help one understand the duality that exists in the Black American experience. It is important to acknowledge the rich and diverse Black diaspora and that I cannot do justice to the diasporic intimacy practices and historic portrayals in one chapter. However, different constituents (activists, the community, academics) utilize these terms widely and favor them for different reasons.

Race and culture impact Black intimacy just like they impact every area of our lives.

> It would not be possible to fully understand the history, current status, and the multiple effects of current…policy in either the UK or the US without placing "race" as a core element of one's analysis. Race is a social construction…Race may function as an absent presence in discussions of markets and standards.[2]

While sex differences are rooted in biology, how we come to understand and perform gender is based on culture. We view culture "as a process through which people circulate and struggle over the meanings of our social experiences, social relations, and therefore, ourselves.".[3]

If we accept the premise that how we perform gender and/or sex roles is based on culture, we must also embrace the notion that intimacy is deeply cultural. Consequently, when choreographing and portraying Black intimacy/love, artists and storytellers (to include directors, filmmakers, producing organizations, playwrights and others) need to take four things into account:

- The difference between intimacy/love and the tensions within a Black couple between their inner intimacy and the outer world.
- History and tropes that shape portrayals of Black love and sex, and how these assumptions and expectations have shaped and limited the role of artists and intimacy professionals, particularly of color.
- How these historical tropes shape audience perception.
- Actors' boundaries within the portrayal.
  One cannot create a consent-based environment or even choreograph a valid and truthful story without consideration of these factors.

The History

Black American intimacy has a long history on the stage and screen. Unfortunately, much work has been intentionally erased and hidden. For example, researchers recently discovered *Something Good – Negro Kiss*, made in 1898, a 29-second clip with a story of Black American intimacy. Starring Saint Suttles and Gertie Brown, it is a film free of racist stereotypes[4] and full of coyness, flirtation, passion and rhythm. While Suttles and Brown were filming this celebration of Black love, white Americans were subjecting African Americans to lynchings, rampant violence, cultural annihilations, fueled by racist propaganda, which many scholars have argued amounted to attempted genocide.[5] The same year *Something Good* was being made the only successful coup d'état on American soil, the Wilmington Massacre, was occurring.[6] During the Wilmington Massacre, white Americans, unhappy with the hard-won new wealth and political power of the African American population, held an insurrection, brutally murdering Black duly-elected politicians and piling up their bodies in the lakes of Wilmington. This example illustrates a paradigm of the push-pull between Black love, as represented in the film, and Black pain, as represented by the actual events that occurred simultaneously.

Such moments illustrate the importance and nuance of culturally specific intimacy choreography. What is at stake in how Black love and intimacy are portrayed is the telling of our history and humanity. One must understand the reality that Black/African Americans endure publicly, while privately being intimate. In this paradox lies hope that is not blind optimism, but courage, promise and possibility that is exhibited in the coupling of two Black people. *To not understand the violence or circumstances out of which Black American culture developed is to overlook key factors in choreographing and storytelling Black intimacy at best, and at worse to reinforce centuries old anti-Black tropes.*

Art As A Reflection of Both Truth and Tropes

When soliciting examples of "Black intimacy," one friend spoke to me about a man sitting between a woman's legs getting his hair cornrowed. Another recalled the sensation of being held at the end of a day and that hug holding an understanding of the fear, code switching and racial negotiations they made that day, but their Black partner "understands and I don't have to explain, it's there in the way they hold me." Others spoke of a shared rhythm, a familiar shorthand with movement, humor or references. All of this, the playfulness, passion, rhythm, the healing tenderness, cannot be divorced from our intimacy. Sometimes when portrayed on screen, we see images of Black lovemaking interspersed with violence and trauma. Beautiful complex stories of Black love often nevertheless have a frantic, violent quality to their depictions of intimacy.

In some cases, this means literal violence interspersed, as in the case of *Queen and Slim* where we see violence as the characters are being intimate, or films where the sex is imbued with trauma, or Black people's sexual pleasure is a punchline and a joke, as with Craig's aunt in *Next Friday*, and the party scene where the character turns into a monster in *Don't Be A Menace*). In other cases, the lack of sexual enjoyment (especially on behalf of the woman) is played up or the scenes are played for humor, as in *Waiting To Exhale*. All of this can serve the othering of Black intimacy. It's not that humor or violence should never take place, but it's a lack of balance to portrayals of other types of Black intimacy that show sensuality, nuance and complexity.

What is so frustrating about flattening tropes or a lack of nuance in Black intimacy is that our lived and story culture is rife with imagery of sensuality, tones of intimacy and consent. Take the description in Toni Morrison's 2007 Book, *Jazz*:

> *Her partner does not whisper in Dorcas' ear. His promises are already clear in the chin he presses into her hair, the fingertips that stay. She stretches up to encircle his neck. He bends to help her do it. They agree on everything above the waist and below: muscle, tendon, bone joint and marrow cooperate. And if the dancers hesitate, have a moment of doubt, the music will solve and dissolve any question…*[7]

In the same way Morrison is framing the rhythm and full nature of the characters' movement with narration in words, one is able to do this with physical movement in intimacy choreography.

Carlton Molette says in *Black Theatre Premise and Presentation*:

> Theatre is a reflection of the time, place, and social strata of those who present it and those for whom it is presented. Insights into the artistic creations of a culture are more likely to be valid when they occur after exposure to the values and the dominant creative motifs of that culture…Sensitivity to art is at least as important as knowledge about it. Cognitive learning that begins in late adolescence or later does not

> produce optimum potential for the development of sensibilities in response to the art of a second culture.[8]

Notice here Molette's emphasis on not only knowledge but a deep engagement with the art and culture to do the work.

A culturally competent intimacy professional, especially one versed in Black feminist scholarship, can be powerful in reshaping storytelling.

> Challenging media portrayals of Black women as mammies, matriarchs, jezebels, welfare mothers, and tragic mulattoes is a core theme in black feminist thought. Author bell hooks contends that Black female representation in the media "determines how blackness and people are seen and how other groups will respond to us based on their relation to these constructed images."[9]

Let's look further at these tropes. There is the "mammy trope:" the Black woman stripped of sexual desire or need but there to serve others. Also in this vein is the "magical negro:" the Black person, male or female, who exists only to serve the needs or desires of the white protagonist or to help them get on the "right path." Think about Olde Mae Brown (Whoopie Goldberg) in *Ghost*, Hattie Mc Daniel in *Gone With The Wind*, or the maids played by Octavia Spencer and Viola Davis in *The Help* (to date Ms. Spencer has been cast as a nurse, maid or cleaner twenty-one times including three Oscar nominated performances).[10] Popular culture has commodified the Black female body as either hyper-sexed or sexless.

The jezebel trope traces back to enslavement when whites used their misunderstandings of Black and African cultural practices (such as dancing or courting practices) to label Black women as sexually deviant, available for the pleasure of white slaveholders and without their own cultural or sexual practices.[11] The "jezebel" motif provides cover for this brutalizing and barbaric treatment, and we see it continue in tropes and the dehumanizing portrayal of Black female sexuality. Examples are rampant, from Sara Baartman to Dorothy Dandridge, to Halle Berry's Oscar-winning performance in *Monster's Ball*, where Hill Collins argued that she played an oversexed jezebel and tragic mulatto at the same time.

In response to these portrayals, respectability politics created the "good wife" and also the "mammy" stereotype. The "good wife" is a go-getting, capitalist portrayal of an achieved career woman, wife and mother. "Prime time television has tended to confine black female roles to white models of 'good wives' and to black matriarchal stereotypes" (Brooks and Herbert,

2006, p. 300). Claire Huxtable of the *The Cosby Show* is a prominent example. While it may seem aspirational, the damage in the portrayal is in the unrealistic standard and often the self-sacrifice that is portrayed. It is not the mammy portrayal because of the "respectable" and "aspirational" elements. Mrs. Huxtable was a beautiful, accomplished lawyer with five children and an OBGYN husband with an erratic schedule. We never saw the Huxtable's employ domestic help, but their house was spotless, their children well taken care of, and the character very amorous toward her husband. While many in the African American community celebrated this portrayal, one has to stop and think about what message about "success" this portrayal sent to Black women. This was an impossible standard and yet this was the way to be seen as "good."

The "good wife" motif becomes a warning for the choreographer. Often used to counter harmful stereotypes of aggressive Black sexuality, we see Black women and femme-identifying people flattened out and virtualized. In avoiding the "jezebel," we can often reduce people with "respectability politics" and lose humor, sensuality and playfulness in trying to avoid these "bad stereotypes." Michael Eric Dyson said, "We are performing Black sensibility, Black intelligence, Black craft."[12] When the intimacy professional is taking on any performance of Black sexuality, particularly when they have a say in intimacy meetings, or a new script development, a deep and nuanced understanding of how these tropes have influenced Western thought and perception, as well as how they have been usurped or reimagined in Black American culture, is important. Black culture is known for reshaping, reclaiming or reimagining. Where possible through the choreography, disrupting racist and stereotypical portrayals and bringing the fullness of the Black intimate should be at the forefront of the intimacy professional's work.

Just like with women and femininity, colonialism is entrenched with othered ideas of men and masculinity that furthered supremacy and exploitation. Black male tropes tend to almost always portray Black masculinity and sexuality as "deviant" or "needing salvation." In some instances, Black males of any orientation are often portrayed as aggressive and dangerous, a threat. Or in other instances, as the male counterpart to the "good wife" motif : capitalist, stripped of cultural markings, often coupled with a non-Black partner. The narrative of the "overcomer" or echoes of self-hate for oneself, one's past and one's culture also tends to exist in portrayals of Black masculinity often paired with "white savior" or "white foil" characters (*The Blindside, White Noise, Dangerous Minds, The Soloist* and *Finding Forester* turn in just a few). Often Black male characters can be stripped of any intimate wants or desires when fulfilling the "magical negro" trope to safely serve a white protagonist (*Bagger Vance, Driving Miss Daisy, Green Mile*).

It is not just the imagery and history that affect the shaping of Black intimacy in performance. For example, Black men suffer from several marginalizing tropes. However, because of the gender bias of some intimacy professionals (especially white females), they can be especially vulnerable to stereotyping and mistreatment, and there is a risk that their concerns and needs will be/are silenced or overlooked.

Consent Work Has a Legacy in Black Studies, Art and Feminism

Because the position of intimacy professional is often thought of inside the field and by many other artists as a role of allyship, awareness or even protection, professionals in the field may overlook their own biases and blind spots around race and entitlement. Many Black practitioners have advocated for consent-based practices for decades (for example Dr. Barbara Ann Teer's *Soul Teer Technology Method*), yet the same gate-keeping practices that have kept many comparable areas of our field unequal exist in the field of intimacy. Relegating independent and smaller companies, especially those run by Black and other people of color, to "emerging" roles is deeply problematic. In addition, while Black identifying coordinators are primarily often put on projects that match their "racialized categories," white choreographers are placed prominently in projects across racial spectrums. This harkens back to a colonial structure of white supremacy.

Intimacy owes both a debt to the practices and advocacy of Black feminist thinkers and storytellers, as well as the foundations laid by Black performance artists in their work. There is a responsibility to include cultural competence and race into the factoring of a consent-based performance space. By understanding the complexities of history, culture, systematic structures and storytelling techniques in intimacy we can revolutionize the space for better storytelling and more broadly for massive cultural change.

Notes

1 Intimacy definition from Pace, Chelsea, et al. *Staging Sex: Best Practices, Tools, and Techniques for Theatrical Intimacy*. Routledge, 2020; with additional work by Kaja Dunn, Bliss Griffin, Ann James, and Laura Rikard.
2 Apple, Michael W. "The Absent Presence Of Race In Educational Reform." *Race And Ethnic City In Education*, vol. 2, No. 1, 1999, pg. 9–16., doi:10.1080/1361332990020102.

3 Brooks, D. E. and Hébert, L. P. (2006). Gender, race, and media representation. 10.4135/9781412976053.n16.
4 Wang, J. (2018). *Silent Film Of Black Couple's Kiss Discovered, Added To National Film Registry.* University of Chicago News, December 12. https://news.uchicago.edu/story/silent-film-black-couples-kiss-discovered-added-national-film-registry.
5 Equal Justice Initiative. (n.d.). *Lynching in America: Confronting the legacy of racial terror.* https://lynchinginamerica.eji.org/report/ /
6 Zinn Education Project. (2022) *Nov. 10, 1898: Wilmington Massacre.* January 30. https://www.zinnedproject.org/news/tdih/wilmington-massacre-2/.
7 Morrison, Toni. (2007) *Jazz.* Knopf Doubleday Publishing Group.
8 Molette, Carlton W. and Barbara J. Molette. (1992) *Black Theatre: Premise and Presentation.* Wyndham Hall Press.
9 hooks, bell (2014) *Black Looks: Race and Representation.* Taylor & Francis.
10 Jones, Ellen E. (2019) "From Mammy to Ma: Hollywood's Favorite Racist Stereotype." BBC Culture, May 31. www.bbc.com/culture/article/20190530-rom-mammy-to-ma-hollywoods-favourite-racist-stereotype.
11 Berry, Daina R. and Leslie M. Harris. (2018) *Sexuality and Slavery: Reclaiming Intimate Histories in the Americas.*
12 Dyson, D. R. M. E. (2022). *Black Theatre: Radical Longevity. MTC and Billie Holiday Theatre.* Manhattan Theatre Club.

Bibliography

Apple, Michael W. (1999) "The Absent Presence Of Race In Educational Reform." *Race And Ethnic City In Education,* vol. 2, No. 1, pg. 9–16, doi:10.1080/1361332990020102.
Berry, Daina R. and Leslie M. Harris. (2018) *Sexuality and Slavery: Reclaiming Intimate Histories in the Americas.*
Brooks, Dwight and Lisa Hébert. (2006) "Gender, Race, and Media Representation." *The SAGE Handbook of Gender and Communication.* Bonnie J. Dow and Julia T. Wood. SAGE Publications, Inc., pp. 297–318. https://dx.doi.org/10.4135/9781412976053.n16.
Brown, Ashley. (2018) "'Least Desirable'? How Racial Discrimination Plays out in Online Dating." *NPR,* 9 January. www.npr.org/2018/01/09/575352051/least-desirable-how-racial-discrimination-plays-out-in-online-dating.
Dyson, D. R. M. E. (2022). *Black Theatre: Radical Longevity. MTC and Billie Holiday Theatre.* Manhattan Theatre Club.
Equal Justice Initiative. (n.d.). *Lynching in America: Confronting the legacy of racial terror.* https://lynchinginamerica.eji.org/report/.
Hill Collins, Patricia. (2004) *Black Sexual Politics: African Americans, Gender, and the New Racism.* Routledge.
hooks, bell (2014) *Black Looks: Race and Representation.* Taylor & Francis.
Jones, Ellen E. (2019) "From Mammy to Ma: Hollywood's Favorite Racist Stereotype." BBC Culture, May 31. www.bbc.com/culture/article/20190530-rom-mammy-to-ma-hollywoods-favourite-racist-stereotype.
Molette, Carlton W. and Barbara J. Molette. (1992) *Black Theatre: Premise and Presentation.* Wyndham Hall Press, 1992.
Morisseau, Dominique. (2022) "Skeleton Crew." January 22. Samuel J. Friedman Theatre.
Morrison, Toni. (2007) *Jazz.* Knopf Doubleday Publishing Group.

North, Dayna Lynne and Kaja Dunn. (2022) "Conversation with Dayna Lynne North of Loudsis Productions." May 5.

Pace, Chelsea, et al. (2020) *Staging Sex: Best Practices, Tools, and Techniques for Theatrical Intimacy*. Routledge, with additional work by Kaja Dunn, Bliss Griffin, Ann James and Laura Rikard.

Vang, T.K. (2015) "Hollywood's Portrayal of Asian American Men: The Sick Man of America." *Academia.edu*, September 12. www.academia.edu/10656855/Hollywoods_Portrayal_of_Asian_American_Men_The_Sick_Man_of_America.

Wang, J. (2018). *Silent Film Of Black Couple's Kiss Discovered, Added To National Film Registry*. University of Chicago News, December 12. https://news.uchicago.edu/story/silent-film-black-couples-kiss-discovered-added-national-film-registry.

Zinn Education Project. (2022) *Nov. 10, 1898: Wilmington Massacre*. January 30. https://www.zinnedproject.org/news/tdih/wilmington-massacre-2/.

A Conversation with Tai Leshaun

Brooke M. Haney

> Tai Leshaun and I worked together on *The Best Man*. Kaja Dunn had done the prep for the scene with Tai, and I was covering for her that day. Tai was playing the character of Jordan, a young Nia Long, and it was her first ever scene of intimacy. Originally, it was supposed to involve a kiss and then the two characters falling into bed. However, when I arrived, Robert Townsend, the director, asked if we could change the choreography. Tai is a 2018 alumni from Marymount Manhattan College, where I had taught for eight years, and while she'd never taken a class with me, Tai recognized my name and made the connection. To have your first scene of intimacy change from a kiss to nearly simulated sex can be intense, so I asked Tai if she would be willing to talk about it.

TAI   Thank you for just being an intimacy coordinator, you don't know how relaxing it is. And I wish this was happening through theater programs, because we were doing all this stuff, and it wasn't there, and it was super uncomfortable. I had that conversation with [a professor at Marymount Manhattan College] when I met with him. There were times where I was kissing people in class, and I wasn't even comfortable. I can't even have a conversation about this or that, because it's written into the sides or written

DOI: 10.4324/9781003410553-18

	into what we got assigned as our scene. You just have to suck it up in your own way, and just be like, I don't feel comfortable, but somehow we're not worrying about consent. It's just we got to do this, you know?
BROOKE	What did the professor say?
TAI	He said how it's changed now. Now they get to choose the type of things they want to work on, what they want to do. Kissing literally only happens when they go to do their scene in class, they don't do it in private rehearsals or anything like that. That way, they are now setting up a space where it is always safe. It's never anything uncomfortable. And you can still also choose to opt out of it. And that's beautiful. It just sucks, because I feel like it took a lot of people going through what they had to for the change to happen. So, I'm glad it's happening now, I just wish I got that opportunity too.
BROOKE	They have also started having intimate scenes choreographed by an intimacy educator, which adds an additional layer of support for the students. On *The Best Man*, you asked to have an intimacy coordinator, right?
TAI	Yeah, literally from the minute I auditioned and found out that I booked it, and they were like, "There is a possibility of nudity." And I was just kind of like, "Um cool. Do we get intimacy coordinators?" And my managers said they should if that's gonna happen, they have to, with SAG.
BROOKE	Actually, currently SAG strongly recommends intimacy coordinators for scenes involving nudity or simulated sex, but it isn't required, so it was great that you asked.
TAI	I was so adamant, because I knew what made me uncomfortable. The line was written as "a steamy moment." I was like, what's the steamy moment? I guess a look? Is it an action? Or what's happening? I have a sentence. I just want to know what it's going to be. And so just knowing at least I could find a way to have some comfort level was just a good feeling.
BROOKE	When the script isn't clear, an intimacy coordinator can help the actor get clarity on what is going to be expected of them on set. You got to talk with Kaja Dunn. Originally, what did she tell you to expect?
TAI	I was told it's just gonna be a kiss, and you fall on the bed. And I was like, that's fine. That's easy.

Kaja also told me you have to have two days' notice if there is going to be something more than just a kiss, where you guys are |

going to be touching or naked. And then I got a text the next day, 'You're gonna have Brooke, but she's amazing. She's gonna be there with you.' And I was like, wait a second, if someone's coming, that means more is happening.

BROOKE   How did the day on set go for you once we started talking about the new choreography?

TAI   When we were having this conversation about what was going to happen, you were there as well. So it wasn't like we're just hearing this. We don't know what to ask, you at least knew to ask for us, or to get clarity for sure on what it was going to be. And then you pulled us aside and asked, 'What do we want to do beforehand? What's going to help us ease into this? How are we going to find just that space and peace?' And it worked out.

BROOKE   Was there anything previously in your career that made you more aware of what to expect?

TAI   When I worked on *Thunder Force*, there was a sleeping scene, and I remember thinking this room is tight. There are a lot of cameras in here, and there's a body attached to the camera. There's someone attached to the sound and everything like that. And I'm like, if this is just for sleeping, and we're not even doing anything. For an actual intimate scene, you have some bodies in there with you, that's a weird thing. And so fast forward to two and a half years later, being in that situation and yeah, there are bodies in here who I don't know their name. There are some people who have seen me in hot pink underwear, who I don't even know.

BROOKE   What was most helpful?

TAI   Just knowing that I could ask questions and ask for what I need, and just know that it's not being a diva. I feel like that's always my worry. I learned that there are things you can advocate for, things you can do, and if you're not happy with stuff, either have your team go ask for you, or you ask.

BROOKE   Was there anything that could have made it better?

TAI   What would have been cool, maybe, is to have been introduced to everyone in the room, even though they're doing their thing.

BROOKE   That's a really good idea. *The Best Man*, compared to many productions, had a larger number of Black creatives—

TAI   It was great that everyone was a person of color, everyone was Black, which doesn't get to happen too frequently. Like the music was great, the level of comfortability was great and it was just such a good feeling. It was great to kind of have them thanking us a lot, being like, 'Thank you guys, you guys were great.'

You know and it was nice to feel appreciated but also just feel appreciated by your own people of color, and the cool thing about *The Best Man* is that there were so many young people as well. Like it wasn't just older 50-, 60-, 70-year-olds or 40-year-olds, you're seeing people from their twenties. This is great to see that our industry is growing, and it's becoming so diverse, age wise, race wise, all of this and just knowing that the people, they care, and they care about making this feel right.

BROOKE   How did that affect the storytelling?

TAI   Having Robert Townsend give us an exercise that had us go through the experience of Black friendship, Black love and everything in between, before we even started shooting, was able to set up the dynamic that was Jordan and Harper. Getting to work through these different dynamics of the Black experience, and discovering each other allowed us to be more active in this first-time experience.

BROOKE   While I'm glad you and I worked well together, Kaja Dunn was the intimacy coordinator who prepared you for the shoot. What's the benefit of having a Black intimacy coordinator to you?

TAI   It's just one thing knowing that we've made it. These industries were always predominantly male, then predominantly white. And to have someone who was Black, who's educated, who's doing this and who's leading this. It's great. You have someone who understands, as Black women, our bodies are built different. I have a very small torso, but I have a bum you know, so like having someone who understands and has knowledge of that and so they can make sure it's happening a certain way that I'm not being overly sexualized because of my body type. They can connect with you and just make you feel safe.

BROOKE   Because there are practical concerns too.

TAI   I kept being like, we need to figure out how to get these pants off my body. It needed to happen at a certain timing, but I'm trying to explain, my hips aren't smooth, my bum's not small. Yeah, I'm trying to figure out how to look sexy and not look like I am struggling to get these off my body. I think, what is it Beyoncé said in one of her songs about, "If you don't jump to put jeans on, you don't feel pain." The Black female body is very different, gets talked about, gets painted, gets used for everything, but it's like, we don't talk about the other side of what comes with that.

And so even knowing Kaja is Black, that's great. I met her on the phone, and she sounded like she was young too. So knowing that was like a young, Black female intimacy coordinator who was able to give me all this information and able to be like, this is everything but even if you have a quick question, Brooke will be there and she can answer anything. But if you still need anything, you have my number and you can still call or text me. That's just, that's someone going above and beyond and caring and making sure that I'm feeling comfortable.

Queer Intimacy   11

*Raja Benz, Leo Mock,
Robbie Taylor Hunt, and
Brooke M. Haney*

The LGBTQIA2S+ community is expansive and the language around it is constantly evolving. Historically, the sexual education that queer folks received in school or from their parents has been limited to nonexistent. While there are exceptions, most of us were raised and assumed straight and cisgendered (cis) until we came out. As a result, any representation of queer intimacy in the media becomes precious to us. It teaches us what to expect, what to do. When a straight lens is put on queer sex, it is stunting for queer folks. In this chapter, I invited Raja Benz, Leo Mock and Robbie Taylor Hunt to join me in writing how to realistically represent and choreograph intimate queer stories. I admit with sadness that the four of us will not even begin to address all the beauty of this community. I only hope that there will be a whole book dedicated to queer intimacy in the near future.

While being straight doesn't preclude you from telling queer stories, having someone who is an expert in telling those stories when intimacy is involved will add credibility to your project and authenticity to your storytelling. In these cases, the IC should be a full creative partner, dramaturging and working with you to choreograph the intimacy.

It is very important to note that queer folks do not have to prove their queerness. Someone can be queer without having ever had sex.

That said, there are lots of queer folks in hetero-facing relationships. If you are an intimacy professional in this position, it is important for you to realize that you benefit from straight passing privilege. Additionally, you should evaluate how much time you spend in queer spaces and how much experience you have with queer intimacy either personally or by education, before calling yourself a specialist in this area. Having the identity doesn't make you an expert. In fact, even a queer person in a queer relationship or relationships doesn't make one an expert in the staging of queer intimacy. Much study and critical thought on the impact of storytelling should be considered when designing choreography.

Those of us writing in this chapter do hold the identities of the intimacy we are writing about, **and** beyond being qualified, working intimacy choreographers, we have done significant study and research in order to also be experts in our specialty. Leo Mock and Raja Benz are also both gender consultants who also have created curriculum on gender for Theatrical Intimacy Education. Robbie Taylor Hunt wrote his Masters thesis on the representations of sex between men on screen and is Chair of the Intimacy Coordination branch committee of BECTU. Knowing the way I was raised, my early relationships and the media I had taken in were straight leaning, when I came out I did extensive study on queerness and intimacy and have in the past several years become sought after as an expert in telling these stories.

Together, we are writing to those of you in our community who are looking to specialize in telling our stories.

Content note: This chapter will discuss, but not detail, sexual assault.

Note: We encourage you to be aware of your positionality as you engage with and digest this learning, and that you keep this in mind while deciding if you are the right IC for a job, alone or with support.

Working with Actors

While we would love it if all queer intimacy was played by actors from our community, that won't always be the case.

From Robbie: While I have worked with straight actors who couldn't care less about performing queer sex, I have also worked with straight actors who have told me that they are particularly nervous about presenting queer sex. Be ready to describe the basics of the sex they will be performing and make no assumptions about what they may know.

If an actor discloses that they are queer, remember that this does not mean that they know everything there is to know about queer sex. Maybe a queer male actor has only had insertive anal sex before or perhaps someone is asexual. What's more, some heteronormative assumptions are baked into queer communities too, and they may come with their own heterosexist ideas of queer sexuality that need questioning just as much as their cis-het peers.

Choreographing T4T
From Raja Benz and Leo Mock

We are devoting this section to both exploring T4T narrative potentiality and doing so through a Trans-informed pedagogical practice informed by the histories of queer and Trans liberation and systems of care. For us, a T4T practice means opportunities for Trans mentorship, collaboration and an abundance of work created by and for Trans folks. In designing some of the first workshops on representations of Trans intimacy, we were inspired by the mixed fluencies and competencies in the room, which reminded us of the many ways we can come to this work and the impacts our lived experiences can have on this work.

Setting the Tone on Set

Embracing Trans-oriented practices ultimately generates a more inclusive field for all. These tools and conversations are pertinent to all performers, which widens our lens to folks who are questioning their gender, and folks who may identify as cis who seek advocacy in feeling their genders honored and well-represented.

With the firestorm of anti-Trans and anti-drag bills, we must have frank conversations with Trans collaborators about safety, especially if we are being brought to an area they are not familiar with and/or where local laws impact our ability to exist publicly. Practicing informed consent means allowing us to make risk-aware decisions. Tell us if the production is willing to break laws for our safety.

The people with the most power on set will set the tone. Framing this work as "industry standard" or "professional expectations" may help in recruiting accomplices.

Getting pronouns right is not the end-all-be-all for supporting Trans artists, *and* misgendering is one of the most frequent harms to Trans folks. Start with private corrections. If those don't work, check in with the Trans actor and offer them options for the next course of action. Document every instance of misgendering or other anti-Trans behavior in your personal reports and connect with allied producers.

On-set resources

Gender consultants can provide support in historical and cultural research, feedback and production-wide training. They can also provide additional advocacy for Trans collaborators, if necessary. A gender consultant could be a useful resource if you don't have a Trans IC for a project, or you want support for an ongoing series with a Trans guest or recurring role.

You might need to factor in extra time for breaks if an actor needs to go further to find an appropriate restroom. Many use needles for HRT, and depending on the duration of the shoot and the length of the shoot days, may need to administer a dose on set. Having accessible sharps containers is a useful safety measure for every set.

Gender-Affirming and Modesty Garments

While sourcing and fitting will largely be under wardrobe's purview, ICs can consult and coordinate between actors and wardrobe. Gender-affirming garments facilitate ease, euphoria or relatedness between a person and their gender. Make sure that actors know they can have chosen undergarments underneath their costume undergarments, and what the parameters of their options are. This can look like boxers under petticoats, tucking and packing under briefs, pride flag socks, tape binding underneath a bra, shapewear beneath baggy clothing, etc.

With any modesty garment, undergarment, prosthetic or intimate prop, we solicit the actor's input and feedback. This supports the actor's physical boundaries as well as their connection to the character, whether they share common genders or not. We avoid unnecessarily gendered product names (shibue/hibue, anything "men's"/"women's" or anything naming genitalia). Have these conversations with actors and folks sourcing garments as early as possible and take notes for wardrobe and props.

Just because a modesty garment is made for a particular combination of genital components does not mean it must be used by performers whose bodies solely reflect those shapes. Individuals may have a genital alliance including internal and external sex organs, size and shape may be affected by hormones, actors may tuck and/or pack to use a particular modesty garment. The incredible variety of bodies (not just Trans bodies, but especially Trans bodies) necessitates a rejection of assumptions about which bodies "match" which modesty garments.

Binding

Binding is flattening and/or displacing chest tissue. Work with wardrobe and the actors to determine what method of binding is best. Some common options include a binder, compression tops or layered sports bras, and tape. With all binding methods, be sure the actors are able to breathe deeply and expand their ribs without pain.

Tucking

Tucking is a way to obscure and flatten external genitalia. While we won't ask if an actor has tucked before, we can ask if they understand the process. Actors can take instructions home to try it in private before doing it on set. If actors are new to tucking, remind them that this may be uncomfortable but should not be painful; if anything hurts, stop, take a break and start over.

Toys and Packers

For some Trans folks, toys (like dildos and strap-ons) and packers are inorganic extensions of the body, and should be treated with the same respect and care as we treat actors' organic bodies. We often treat prosthetics as a de-sexualized, lower stakes alternative to actors' genitalia. It is important to remember that packers and toys are not prosthetics, and that the line between them is fluid enough that they may hold similar contexts to genitalia for Trans actors.

Because oral sex and stimulation on a packer, toy or other gear is, for many, "real sex," we use masking techniques just as we would for organic genitalia. You may want to consider isolating shots where the prop is not yet secured to the body to reduce the overlap between "real" and "simulated" sex. Additionally, strap-ons can be worn by any person; for those who do not enjoy using their own genitalia in penetrative intercourse, a strap may offer a more affirming alternative.

On packers: "Packer" generally refers to any object that represents, literally or figuratively, the shape, weight and some uses of a phallus (and sometimes testicles). The particular context and action of the scene may call for a hard, soft and/or STP (stand-to-pee) packer, fabric packer or DIY packer. These can be held to the body with harnesses, jock-straps, tape, packing or standard underwear, many of which offer high coverage or wide straps that work well to mask tape lines, barriers and modesty garments.

Nudity

It is useful to define nudity when working with all actors, and especially with Trans actors. Personal definitions may differ from legal definitions. For example, many regions have "topless laws" specific to women. Any team members who are perceived as women (whether correctly or incorrectly) may be affected by these laws. This is an especially important conversation when working in public or outdoor sets.

Take time to affirm actors whose bodies are in conflict with those legal definitions, and collaborate with them toward clear and specific safety plans if public nudity puts them in legal or physical danger. Consider including toys, packers and prosthetics in your definitions of nudity, and offer coverage between takes.

Choreography Considerations

T4T intimacy is often a process of rewriting, rather than adapting, the sexual scripts we were taught. For many Trans people, this means exploring inventive ways to use the parts they have, discovering new sensations that result from their body's conversation with hormones. Discovery, both of likes and dislikes, is plentiful in Trans intimacies, and especially T4T intimacies. Catalog what assumptions you hold around Trans sex, and know that many of us enjoy disrupting those assumptions. That said, the boundaries of the actor will supersede the character's.

Some stories of Trans intimacy we don't see often enough: mutual hair maintenance, lavishing bottom growth, trading clothes, muffing, slow exploration.

Final Thoughts

We hope you leave this with quintessentially queer curiosity, and continue to question your knowledge and practices (a deeply Trans practice). We ask that you find ways to incorporate Trans inclusive pedagogy into your daily life, and that you continue to be in conversation with us. Trans folks have always been and will always be leaders in putting self-determination and autonomy at the forefront of creation. Despite an increase of Trans visibility in media (in no small part to ongoing political attacks), we are not yet in a time of true Trans inclusion – particularly in the ways in which we make our media. The reach and educational potential of media being what it is, we cannot understate the significance a Trans-competent field of intimacy coordination could make.

Choreographing Lesbian Sex
From Brooke M. Haney

Cheryl Clarke, in her essay "Lesbianism: An Act of Resistance," writes: "For a woman to be a lesbian in a male-supremacists, capitalist, misogynist, racist, homophobic, imperialist culture, such as that of North America is an act of resistance." Later she continues: "Historically, this culture has come to identify lesbians as women, who over time, engage in a range and variety of sexual–emotional relationships with women. I, for one, identify a woman as a lesbian who says she is." For the purpose of this section, I would like to amend that to say that I (Brooke), for one, identify a **person** as a lesbian who says **they** are. I make this change to define what kind of simulated sex I will be writing about. I want to acknowledge that I am a white, pansexual, most often femme presenting, genderqueer human in a currently monogamous, lesbian-facing relationship. The kinds of stories I'm most excited about choreographing are what I would consider an expansive idea of lesbianism and queerness in comparison to what we currently see on TV and in film, and I would consider these stories an act of resistance. My bias will certainly come through in this section.

> There are lots of ways to express emotional and physical intimacy, and lesbian bed death is a myth, please don't perpetuate it.

Let's be clear, you do not have to have a vagina to be a woman or a femme. That said, in the interest of specificity, and because of femme-for-femme erasure by the heteropatriarchy, most (but not all) of the sex I will be writing about in this section will be about vagina owners. After all, what lesbian couple hasn't been asked how they have sex with an air of incredulity? This confusion seems to come from the fact that so many straight folks don't understand how someone could possibly have sex without a penis.

Historical Considerations

If you are researching a project, or simply want some inspiration, the Lesbian Herstory Archives is a great place to start. Historical considerations around lesbian sex are incredibly instructive. For example, in the US in the 1940s, 1950s and 1960s, lesbians hung out in secret bars. The culture was very butch/femme/kiki. Butches topped, femmes were pillow princesses and kiki girls switched and were judged for it. Conforming to your role gave a feeling of belonging. At this time, lesbians and Trans men were being stopped on the streets by the police and checked to make sure they were wearing three pieces of women's clothing. If not, they were arrested for cross-dressing. Sometimes these police officers pulled down their underwear, "using the law as an excuse for street-level sexual assault and sexual humiliation" (History.com, 2019). Additionally, there was little to no racial integration in the speakeasy type bars lesbians frequented. This may feel like distant history, but the 1960s weren't that long ago. Taking a look at what was going on politically and culturally at the time your story is set will tell a lot about how lesbians expressed affection publicly and privately and how they experienced sexual harm.

Pre-Production

When meeting with the director, in addition to the questions I regularly ask, I like to ask what their goal is in how we craft the intimacy. When realism or greater representation of the queer experience is part of their answer, I'm thrilled. I listen to what they are thinking about for the choreography, and, when welcomed, make suggestions around how to make it more original, nuanced or realistic.

Lesbian Sex Acts

I have a bingo card of sex positions I haven't seen, or have rarely seen, in film or on TV that I want to choreograph. While I won't include it here, I will discuss some of the basic ways in which lesbians have sex.

Oral: This is a common depiction of lesbian sex, probably because it's delightful, and easy for straight folks to understand, as they know how it works. Face sitting is a particularly popular form of oral sex that can incorporate power dynamics. When getting actors into position, be careful that the actor on top doesn't knee their partner. A discreetly placed yoga block covered with a sheet or sitting back a bit on the "giver's" chest can take pressure off the hips and knees especially between takes. Face sitting is also an excellent position for group sex as both partners are still highly available.

Manual: Perhaps most commonly called fingering, while manual sex may include digital penetration, there are thousands of nerve endings in the clitoris and caressing or massaging the labia can be quite pleasurable. Most vagina owners don't go from zero to 100 the minute someone's hand goes down their pants. Consider incorporating outer vulva play rather than going straight to penetration – eye contact and the way the receiving character breathes will express a lot: quickly lowered or raised gaze, a quick inhale and tensing may imply penetration, while direct eye contact, slow measured breathing that turns to light panting might indicate a labia massage followed by teasing of the clit.

Penetrative: Penetrative sex, other than manual/digital, may happen with a toy, with a penis if the lesbian in question has a lady penis (or giant clit, or whatever she calls it) or with a strap-on, traditional, thigh or other. The vagina can triple in size when aroused, so fisting is also a popular method for those looking for intense sensation. While a traditional strap-on might lend itself to hetero positioning, if your story involves penetration by hand, foot, toy or something else, consider the positioning of bodies and try to avoid parallels. Putting bodies off to one side or perpendicular to each other is one of my favorite ways to queer sex.

Anal: Just because there is no penis involved doesn't take anal sex off the table. Lesbians still experience sensation in that area. So rimming, digital penetration and penetration with toys are all possible scenarios.

Masturbation: Mutual masturbation is an incredible way to show deep intimacy and trust.

Scissoring: Sure, some lesbians do scissor, but if you believed straight-created lesbian porn or water cooler talk, you'd think this is the missionary position of lesbian sex. After all, if straight folks insert a penis into a vagina, then two vagina owners must mash their genitals together too. In reality, it is more fetishized than it is common practice. This position is easy to mask, and while there are various bodily orientations for the creative scissorer, the one folks most think of is difficult to choreograph off center. So barriers become very important. I like to use a small ball or folded yoga mat and mask it with the legs.

Toys: Popular toys include a hitachi wand or other personal vibrator, labia spreaders, strap-ons and dildos, butt plugs, anal beads, bondage gear, impact tools or any other kink toys. As a result of toxic masculinity, a woman using a toy, especially a vibrator, is often portrayed as an affront to a man's sexual prowess. This insecurity exists much less in lesbian culture and toys are considered part of the fun. So, include them in your storytelling, if only tossed to the side in a scene.

Choreographic Considerations

Now that we have a menu of sex acts to simulate, let's discuss queering our lens. I love looking at lesbian art for inspiration for my work. Avoid the straight gaze by choreographing scenes that don't mimic or reinforce a heteronormative story around sex, whether it be parallel lines with one character on top, a story arc that reinforces climax as the end of sex or other such tropes. Of course these can be part of your storytelling, simply go further as well. Because it doesn't necessarily end at a climax, queer sex often (but not always) lasts a long time – sometimes comically long – only ending when someone finally taps out. Find creative ways to show the length and endurance of the experience.

Expand on your positions by asking: are the characters standing, sitting, lying down? Are they on a bed, the floor, a chair, table or bench? Bathtub? Shower? Toilet? What is their orientation to each other? I'll say it again – perpendiculars are interesting.

Make use of all the ingredients of intimacy choreography (*Staging Sex*) and remember that extremes and opposites are interesting.

When a character has sex either with the same person over multiple scenes, or with different characters over the course of a film, episode or season this is an opportunity to show lots of variety. How is their sex different with different partners? Creating different dynamics between pairings allows nuanced character development. How does their sex life change over time with the same partner or partners? When is it boring, exciting, new, uncomfortable, thrilling? This can be a benefit of having one intimacy coordinator who oversees a TV series for example. Then, as directors change episode to episode, the IC can track the trajectory of the intimacy to make sure the story is consistent, growing and alive.

Finally, make it awkward, uncomfortable, silly, etc. Rarely is sex flawlessly sexy.

Other Considerations

Boundaries

"They'll be fine, they're both girls," is problematic on so many levels. Every actor deserves the space to articulate their boundaries every time. The assumption that someone's gender automatically makes them safe or unsafe is dangerous. Besides, ICs are not there to protect actors from perpetrators, we are there to empower actors to express their boundaries so that everyone is on the same page and can consent to creating brave, compelling art.

Barriers

Do I still need one? Yes, if you're staging simulated sex, you do. Remember that a barrier is to reduce sensation and prevent the exchange of body fluids. Hot tip: when I've had a vagina owner that is particularly afraid of their own body's aptitude for the release of fluids, a tampon can be a layer of added protection and peace of mind under the barrier.

Safer Sex

It is a fallacy that lesbians don't need to worry about STIs (or unplanned pregnancy for that matter, depending on their anatomy). When possible, give nods to safer sex practices in your projects. Common practices include latex gloves (black ones are sexy), condoms (for dildos or any other sex toy that fits inside a condom) and dental dams, which can be created DIY from plastic wrap, gloves or a condom (I've actually choreographed that last one).

Blood

Normalize sex with blood. If both people in a relationship have periods, and want to have a lot of regular sex, blood will be involved. So when can you incorporate towels, shower sex, tampon removal (I see you *I May Destroy You*) into your storytelling?

If using blood, work closely with wardrobe, props and SPFX: check to see if any of your actors have a vasovagal response (fainting at the sight of blood), ask about allergies or sensitivities (latex, chocolate, sugar), use water for rehearsals and plan for extra costumes and supplies.

Kink

Because queer folks have historically not had representation of what sex could look like for them, it makes sense that we are open to a large definition as well as lots of exploration. This kind of curiosity combined with communication (which is conditioned into folks assigned female at birth) is the perfect foundation for kink. Perhaps that's why people ask if being kinky makes you queer (google it). To be clear, it doesn't. Are we actually more likely to be kinky, or has our lack of representation given us the opportunity to discover it with more ease? Perhaps the repression, in some ways, has been freeing.

Choreographing Queer Male Sex
From Robbie Taylor Hunt

While I often refer to "queer male sex," some of what I discuss is relevant to non-binary characters and actors, such as those that have sex with queer men. Some discussion is not exclusive to queer male sexuality, e.g. anyone regardless of their gender, sexuality or body can have anal sex as the insertive or receptive partner (which may include the use of a strap-on).

Sexual Dramaturgy

Pre-production meetings are where I have dramaturgical discussions about queer sex on screen. If the goal is to present realistic queer male sex, I offer what we might include to achieve that. I'm struck even working with queer male directors and writers how certain aspects of queer sex get left behind in the conceptualization of these scenes. Frankly, I think this is because we're so unused to seeing them represented properly that we have had the (straight) wool pulled over even our (gay) eyes. Here's some main areas to question.

Anal Sex and Sexual Positioning Roles

Although it is a key part of many queer men's lives, not all have anal sex. Check whether there's an assumption that the choreographed sex has to culminate in anal sex. As with all sex, there's a heteronormative social expectation that true sex must include penetration.

If there is anal sex, reflect on which character is the top (sexually insertive partner) and which character is the bottom (sexually receptive partner). Another heterosexist import into queer male sexuality is an expectation that a younger, shorter, slimmer, more feminine and/or less hairy character will be the bottom and an older, taller, more muscular, masculine and/or hairy character will be the top. If a character's sex life spans more than one moment on screen, remember that many queers have versatile sex (adopting both insertive and receptive sexual positions).

> Versatile sex is showcased wonderfully in the sex montage sequence in *It's a Sin* (2021). *Tales of the City* (2019) presents beefier, hairier Mouse bottoming with younger boyfriend Ben.

Lubrication

As the anus doesn't self-lubricate, lubrication is often required during anal sex to help to ease the insertion and increase the pleasure for both parties (particularly the receptive partner). Including the application of a lubricant helps a scene seem realistic to queer viewers. If we cut into the scene mid-sex, perhaps there is a bottle of lube nearby. "But my scene isn't modern so they wouldn't have lube." Incorrect! K-Y Jelly was sold as a "surgical aid" in 1904, Vaseline was patented in 1872, the Japanese used tororo-jiru – a substance made from mashed yams – in the Edo period (1603–1863), ancient Greeks and Romans used olive oil, and in China lube was made from boiling red seaweed as early as 600 BC (Rowland, 2023). Spit as lube can be enough for some, but usually isn't ideal. If this is the only option then there should be a substantial amount; consider collaborating with SFX or VFX.

Using proper lube, spit lube or no lube will affect the sexual response of the characters, particularly the bottom; without proper lubrication we may expect larger reactions from the receptive partner and perhaps some performance of discomfort.

Physical Preparation

Digital stimulation of the anus helps to relax it, preparing it for penetration of a strap or penis. Here, a finger is inserted into the anus and can stimulate the prostate (for people assigned male at birth). A lubricated finger can also apply lube to the anus. Oral stimulation, or "rimming," can help to relax and lubricate the anus and is enjoyable due to the many nerve endings present.

Douching and Cleanliness

Considering whether the receptive partner is relatively clear of feces is often a factor in queer men's sex lives. A receptive partner may douche (spray water into their anal cavity to expel fecal residue) before anal sex. However, some men consider their diet before bottoming and simply defecate before sex. Regardless, if two characters have been at dinner then stumble home to immediately start having sex, you can bet some queer eyebrows will be raised. I'm not suggesting that we start every directorial meeting ready to pitch a full douching sequence (tempting as it is), just be mindful of it. For example, this issue is dealt with in *The Last of Us* (2023) by Murray Bartlett's character telling his partner to "go take a shower" before a jump forward in time to the intimate scene.

The Receptive Partner's Orgasm

My previous research has indicated that depicting the receptive partner reaching orgasm (before, during or after anal sex) is very rare on screen (Taylor Hunt, 2022). The insertive partner's orgasm signaling the end of sex links to typical heteronormative centering of the man's orgasm. Some receptive partners in anal sex can orgasm just from anal stimulation and many will orgasm through manual stimulation of their penis (self-stimulating or from their partner) during anal sex. Question a director on what signals the end of a sex scene: could the receptive partner orgasm too?

> Rare examples of the receptive partner orgasming include British independent film *The Weekend* (2011) and independent French drama-thriller *Stranger by the Lake* (2013).

Positions

Anal sex can happen in many positions. Face-to-face with the insertive partner on top (hands to ankles, hands to thighs, forehead to forehead), from behind (receptive partner on hands and knees, kneeling but upright, flat against the bed), with the receptive partner on top (facing either direction, with their knees against the bed or in a squat), standing from behind, standing face-to-face with the insertive partner holding the receptive partner, spooning and more! Unimaginative heterosexual constructions of queer male sex during cinematic and televisual history have led to a disproportionate amount of sex from behind. Get creative!

Practical and Choreographic Considerations

Many choreographic considerations are inherent to the above dramaturgical points, but below are some other practical factors.

External Genitalia

If you're working with two cisgender male actors, there are two sets of external genitalia, which can prove difficult when choreographing simulated sex that maintains performers' comfort without genitals getting in the way. For example, with the receptive partner on top of the insertive partner, it can be tricky to remain in the correct position, have both partners' external genitals present (in modesty garments), have an external barrier and protect the insertive partner's genitals from being pressed against firmly, particularly in representations of deeper or vigorous sex.

There are choreographic tricks of course – such as bracing the upper-front of the insertive partner's thighs against the receptive partner's buttocks – but this is also where sexual positions may affect how modesty garments are used to deal with two sets of external genitalia. Some garments keep the genitals pressed down and slightly tucked under (e.g. Intimask's Vega Strapless Thong), whereas others keep the genitals more forward (e.g. Intimask's Shield Pouch). Either can be useful in different situations; for example, in the aforementioned choreographic position, a Vega Strapless Thong helps to purposefully keep the genitals partially tucked away for the insertive partner, while the receptive partner having their genitals forward in the Shield Pouch keeps their testicles from getting caught between bodies.

The Anus

The anus is sensitive and should be protected from touch during simulated sex. While in reality the character may have their buttocks more spread to allow access to the anus, this may not be necessary for the actors – depending on sexual position and camera angle – which allows the buttocks to provide a level of protection.

I have often used Intimask's Vega Strapless Brief (with the silicone rear barrier) for the receptive partner, although sometimes have trimmed it to see more buttock. I have also added a DIY silicone barrier to the tail of Intimask's Vega Strapless Thong when most of the buttocks need to be seen.

Receptive Partner's Reaction

To describe the sensation of realistic receptive anal sex to actors I use phrases such as: intense, euphoric, internal, a feeling of fullness, overwhelming, stimulating and/or releasing. However, everyone's experiences are different, and we must consider what makes sense for the character.

Here is an example of a typical map I may give an actor for the journey through a moment of anal insertion: as insertion begins there is an overwhelming feeling where it may feel nearly too much, breath is held and higher in the chest, there are purposeful out-breaths to relax the body, inhales deepen as the feeling becomes more internal and stimulating, some vocalization increases alongside the breath, there is still some sense of suspension, once the penis is more fully inside there is relaxing and releasing with more full outbreath and a steadying of the breath. There may be a deeper, fuller vocal and physical reaction with further thrusting. So much is sold with breath – do not neglect breathwork! A good insertive partner would be reading the receptive partner's physical cues (eye contact, breath, nods, smiles) if there isn't explicit dialogue (see *Red White and Royal Blue* [2023] for sequences of receptive anal sex including these cues).

While anal sex can have moments of discomfort, disproportionately showcasing pain for the receptive partner is part of a homophobic inability to see queer male sex – particularly the penetration of a man – as solely pleasurable, joyful or loving.

> **From Robbie:** A frank aside about protecting yourself if you are an LGBTQIA+ intimacy coordinator. I have occasionally found it difficult to discuss performers' boundaries that are obviously based on them not wanting to be presented as queer or perform sex acts that are associated with queerness. Of course all boundaries are valid, and confronting homophobic reasoning behind actors' boundaries creates

> an inherent coercion that is at odds with our work. However, remaining neutral and professional toward an actor's underlying discomfort around queerness has felt challenging to me. I encourage you to fully acknowledge this difficult feeling, give yourself time to decompress, and focus your self-care practices if you are working with performers where this dynamic is evident.

Resources

TransTape: Instructions online for binding and packing
Unclockable: Tuck kits with online instructions
Fucking Trans Women by Mira Bellwether: A 2010 zine that offers comprehensive exploration of sex with and for pre- and non-op Trans women.
Trans Sex by Lucie Fielding: Primarily a healthcare perspective, centering pleasure-focused Trans sex and challenging dominant narratives around cis-centric sexual scripts.
Trans/Love & Gendered Hearts edited by Morty Diamond: A multitude of perspectives on Trans intimacies, exploring how gender and sexuality can inform and affirm one another.
Cruising Utopia, the Then and There of Queer Futurity by José Muñoz :Manifesto on queer futurities, sexual politics and dream-work imagining how our communities may thrive for generations to come.
Disclosure: A documentary produced and directed by Sam Feder. It is an in-depth look at Hollywood's depiction of transgender people and the impact of their stories on transgender lives and American culture.
Lesbian Herstory Archives: New Yorkers can visit these archives in person, and there is an incredible amount of digital resources on the website: photos, periodicals, 3,000 digitized oral herstory cassettes and more.

Bibliography

Clark, Cheryl. (2015) "Lesbianism: An Act of Resistance." *This Bridge Called My Back*, edited by Gloria Anzaldúa and Cerrie Moraga, State University of New York Press, Albany.
History.com. "How Dressing in Drag Was Labeled a Crime in the 20th Century." (2019) *History.com*, June 25, https://www.history.com/news/stonewall-riots-lgbtq-drag-three-article-rule.

Taylor Hunt, Robbie (2022). *"Why don't you have the sex that you want to have?" Investigating how homonormativity shapes queer men's sexual attitudes, behaviours, and representations.* Open Access Te Herenga Waka-Victoria University of Wellington. Thesis. https://doi.org/10.26686/wgtn.21391044

Rowland, S. (2023) "The History of Lube." https://getmaude.com/blogs/themaudern/the-history-of-lube.

A Conversation with Becca Blackwell

Brooke M. Haney

> Becca Blackwell is a legend in the queer and Trans theatre community in New York City, from Broadway to off-off Broadway, and they work a lot on TV and in film. They were in season four, episode eight of *High Maintenance,* working with intimacy coordinator Alicia Rodis. Both Becca and I are passionate about realistic representation of queer intimacy, so we sat down to talk about this episode and the representation of queer sex in general.

BECCA   I think as queers, because we don't have a world where we are seeing ourselves grown up, because we don't have elders, queer parents or tons of queer relatives, we can't, you know, see ourselves represented. We have very little media. So we're kind of in a wonderful arrested development of childhood, which makes our relationships sometimes very immature and also kind of beautiful.

BROOKE   Before I started doing intimacy coordinating work, I had to do a lot of research on queer sex because no matter how gay I am, I know that I'll never have every queer experience. I recognized that the queer media that I saw on TV or theatre or film, most of it was still made through a straight lens. Because we've all ingested so much of that gaze, it is conditioned into us. I had to

	step back and question, what could this actually look like? And then I have to hope I have a creative team that wants to hear my input.
BECCA	Right. When we did our *High Maintenance* episode [season four, episode eight], I remember I had to act like I was giving head to another person who had a vagina, another masc person. And I remember they kept being like, you have to do this with your head (nods). I was like, it looks like I'm giving them a blow job.
BROOKE	But it actually looks different on the monitor than it feels sometimes.
BECCA	It was great because *High Maintenance*, you know, is run by queers. So we were really wanting to show, what does it look like to have two masculine people show intimacy that are vagina owners, because we never see that. Like, no one even knows what to do with two bull dikes or like Trans masc type people. That was something that was really important for me as an artist, because I was like I want to show that being really flippant and not explained.
BROOKE	So many folks would benefit from that. Seeing yourself represented for the first time is wildly powerful, especially realistically and casually.
BECCA	It was one of those episodes where the people who loved it the most were people who were queer, who'd never seen themselves. This is this person's life and they have sex with this person, and they also have sex with a cis femme person.
BROOKE	Alicia Rodis was your intimacy coordinator on *High Maintenance*, right?
BECCA	Yeah, she was very sweet. That episode, I had three sex scenes.
BROOKE	Tell me about them.
BECCA	I had one where I was totally naked with a strap on, and I was like laying on top of this straight woman, essentially. And she was older than me. She was super cool. And I had to roll around in bed with her, kiss her back and like – this shows you how not queer it was – they were like, here's the dildo. It was a purple sparkly dildo. This was not bought by a queer person.
BROOKE	Nope.
BECCA	This was bought by a straight man who wanted his girlfriend to wear it to fuck him in the butt. And everyone was like, "Do you feel comfortable?" And I was like, "Oh, it's fine. Look at the actress. She looks like a straight woman. She probably went and bought it."

BROOKE Yeah, her character bought it.

BECCA Yeah, that was the funny moment, but [Alicia] was like, "Are you okay with this? We want to make sure that you feel empowered." And I'm like, who cares? Right after that, my character is like calling their ex-lover. They're using sex as kind of a means of barreling through feelings.

BROOKE I appreciate that Alicia checked with you. Was your experience that Alicia was mostly there to advocate for the actors? Was she also choreographing or was she letting you two come up with it? Or you four, I guess, over the course of the episode?

BECCA It was a little bit of both. The scene between the Trans masc guy and I, it was really intimate and it was in a loft. So, there was just the camera guy in this corner and then the two of us on this little bed. And then Alicia and the director and the line producer were underneath the loft, looking at the screen. So it was like really weird, you know? And the camera guy was so sweet, trying to be like, you know, neutral man. Like they're just totally supposed to be like, "I'm casual."

BROOKE Yeah, I feel sad when I come onto a set and there's a bit of tension and someone is immediately telling me, "I promise, I'm not a problem." I'm always like, "Dude. I don't think you're a problem. I assume that y'all are well-intentioned." I'm simply here to facilitate a conversation so nothing happens unexpectedly. A lot of harm happens because of broken expectations, and communication can preempt a lot of that.

BECCA Of course there are some assholes, but I assume most people are not that, right?

BROOKE Exactly – of course there are some, but most folks aren't. Did you know the actor that played the Trans masc guy?

BECCA Our community is so small that I like know every single Trans masc actor. Of course I know them, because there's only like 12 of us.

BROOKE Yeah, and I would assume it's rare that you get to do something together. You're more often competing for the role.

BECCA Yeah, it was great. I mean, we had a really sweet little scene right before the sex scene of us getting stoned in the tree and being flirty and it was nice because, again, there's not a lot of opportunity.

BROOKE When you do get the opportunity to work on queer and Trans projects, do they feel realistic to you?

BECCA   Yeah, I feel like the ones I've worked on are pretty realistic. Right. People running around in their panties. You know, even like right after we have sex, there's an immediate like putting on your underwear. So you're not like sitting down on your couch, putting your goosey coos all over the place.

BROOKE   What has surprised you?

BECCA   Something I didn't realize until I was passing as this (gestures at themselves), participating in more like gay male sex, there's a whole different dynamic that's happening here, a whole different way of engaging.

BROOKE   Why was that experience surprising?

BECCA   We never see ourselves represented. I don't think the entirety of gay sex is represented in a way that's realistic. I think we try to make sex really like a little more accessible and clean, not as messy not as complicated. The thing is like sex is really confusing and dirty, and each person's gonna have it very differently and they're bringing all their history to it. They're bringing all their repression to it. You know and then you're just surprised at how many people just aren't even connected to their body.

BROOKE   There should be more actor training around intimacy. Actors should know that they're responsible for knowing and articulating their boundaries and for their self-care practices after a project. Also, to do really good intimacy work, you need to have really good discipline of your body. We're going to ask you to put your body in all these different positions. We're going to ask it to look relaxed, we're going to ask it to look tense and you're going to have to be able to do all that consistently.

BECCA   Yeah, and you're going to have to hit shots.

BDSM

Olivia "Troy" Troy

12

> When season one of *Bonding* came out, the BDSM community reacted in frustrated disappointment at another opportunity for representation squandered. Rather than continuing on with their same plan for season two, the production hired Troy, a BDSM expert, as their intimacy coordinator, including inviting her into the writers room, and that changed everything. This is a top example of why I wrote this book. Simply bringing in any IC wouldn't have made the kinds of change that Troy was able to make, because not every IC has an expertise in BDSM. When the right IC is on a production, our work goes beyond boundaries and consent to propel the storytelling. What a treat it is to have Troy write the chapter on BDSM for this book.

The one thing I say about intimacy coordinators is that there's no such thing as "the best IC" so much as finding the intimacy professional that's best *for your production*. That means a trained professional who, ideally, shares the identities or lived experiences of the actors or of the stories being told. It's also important to find an IC who can support the creative and administrative needs specific to your production. For example, consider if your actors or director need additional support with intimate choreography, or if your show will require numerous nudity and simulated sex riders. When interviewing candidates, you may want to ask if the IC has a particular specialty or what types of projects make best use of their skillset.

My journey into intimacy coordinating began with my work as a professional BDSM practitioner. Consent, scene negotiation, scene choreography and understanding power dynamics are integral to BDSM play, so applying those skills from 15-plus years of experience in kink to supporting intimate scenes in theatre, film and television was a natural evolution. When I started doing the work, few – myself included – had even heard of "intimacy coordinators" much less recognized how necessary the role was for creating a safer environment for vulnerable work.

Consequently, my early production credits included titles such as "BDSM adviser," "intimacy ritualist," "technical consultant" and "BDSM consultant." While these roles all relied on my BDSM expertise, the heart of the work was often quite similar to what would ultimately become the responsibilities of an intimacy coordinator. As a BDSM consultant, my job was to make sure that the BDSM representation was authentic, the details (production design, wardrobe, content and choreography) were accurate, and that the actors in the scene were informed, consenting and comfortable with what the story required.

As intimacy coordinating gained more visibility and traction on sets, I enrolled in an IC training program so that I might continue my work beyond BDSM-related scenes. Although I've worked on dozens of film and television productions as an intimacy coordinator, I'm best known for my work on projects with characters and stories that exist outside the conventions of heteronormative, "vanilla" sexual identities and expressions. As an IC, I prioritize projects with storylines involving BDSM or sex work, women-centered narratives and shows with Q/POC performers. While, on some projects, my work as an IC is similar to what I do as production consultant, it's been my experience that I have more creative latitude and input as a BDSM consultant than as an intimacy coordinator for a scene with kink elements, though typically production consultants have much more limited scope, sway and pay on set than intimacy coordinators.

How my responsibilities in consulting or coordinating roles balance out changes with each production. As the BDSM consultant for *Billions*, the Showtime series starring Paul Giammati as US Attorney Chuck Rhoades, who frequents fetish clubs, sessions with professional dominatrices and plays with his wife Wendy, a tough hedge fund psychiatrist-turned-performance coach who tops him at home, my role was largely advising the actors and executing showrunners' Brian Koppleman and David Levien's vision for each scenario. As a passionate advocate for representation ("Nothing about us without us!"),

I also made sure that background performers for kink scenes were hired from the BDSM community and that the sets reflected realistic kink spaces.

As consulting producer for Netflix's *Bonding*, my role extended to sharing in the writing of season two of the series, as well as sourcing set dressing and props from NYC's working BDSM studios, and casting real-life professional dominatrices for the dungeon scenes. On set, I supported director Rightor Doyle with choreography and blocking, in addition to teaching the leads specific character and implementing techniques relevant to their scenes. I'm very proud to say that when the kink community is asked which shows have the most authentic and accurate BDSM representation and portrayals, the shows I've worked on are consistently at the top of those lists.

Preproduction

As an IC working on BDSM scenes, my primary job is to understand the director's vision for the scene and make sure the requirements fall within the actor's boundaries and comfort level. At times, my knowledge and experience in BDSM is helpful in coming up with viable alternatives should a scripted action not align with an actor's abilities or limits, much in the same way I would for certain scripted sexual acts or positions. I also have deep knowledge of the types of gear used in BDSM scenes, which is helpful in supporting props when it comes to implement suggestions, like finding a paddle that looks or sounds imposing but isn't likely to cause harm. I also support production in making sure the crew understands the scene taking place and that the actions are consensual. Depending on the acts required, particularly scenes where impact is involved, I may also confer with the stunt department to provide protective padding as well as wardrobe to ensure that the actors' costumes can accommodate the padding.

Whenever I read a BDSM scene in a script for a project I'm ICing, the first thing I do is identify what the scene requires based on the script. This includes determining if there are any props involved and what the actor may need to know about their use in order to convincingly execute the scene. Next, I'll talk with the director about their vision for the scene, including what the actors will be wearing, if there is any nudity or simulated sex, which will require that a nudity rider also be prepared. We will also discuss whether the scene should take place on a closed set (SAG guidelines state that any scene with a nudity rider be filmed on a closed set, but scenes with BDSM are at the production's discretion).

Coordinating with Other Departments

Another important consideration is if there is any physical impact (e.g. spanking, whipping, slapping) then it should be clear whether the intention is to show the actual impact or only the gesture of the swing, so that the consenting actor can be prepped accordingly. If there is to be actual physical contact, then additional departments (stunts, fights, SPFX) will need to be consulted for staging support. In my experience, it's best to consult with those departments regardless, so that everyone is prepped and prepared should the plans change (e.g. a no-impact scene becomes an implied impact scene and the actor needs protective padding as a safety measure). Similarly, if a scene requires any restraints, such as rope, cuffs, chains or bondage gear, not only is it vital for the IC to check in with the actor about their comfort with being restrained in the specified material, with consideration of how long they would need to maintain the bondage, the IC should also be prepared to support the director, actors, wardrobe, props, stunts, fights and special effects in choreography and execution on the day.

Stunts, SPFX and other departments should be advised about the performer's limits and boundaries when consulted for BDSM scenes. There can be a higher level of vulnerability with these kinds of scenes, especially if it's new territory for the actor, and the actor may consider having the IC present for those production consultations. The IC should also inform wardrobe if the scene requires any padding or other costume disruption. If the actor is to be nude for the scene, the departments will want to discuss with the director how to best achieve the vision for the scene while maintaining the actor's safety and comfort.

Actor Prep

When talking with actors, it's important to remember that many people do not have any familiarity or experience with BDSM. Actors need to know what they're saying yes to, especially in scenes that contain acts that rely on power dynamics, entail use of specific props or require choreography that the actor has no movement experience with, such as handling an impact toy or being in a restricted or confined space. The IC, in communication with the director, must make sure the actor clearly understands the scope of the scene and is empowered with language to ask questions and convey any concerns.

For example, I worked on a scene that took place in a BDSM club and a dominatrix invites a character to experience being dominated. The plan was to have the actor, a Black woman, be pressed against a metal cage, but when that vision was described to her, she expressed discomfort with the racial history and connotations of that prop, and asked that we avoid any positioning or gear that might be a signifier of slavery or that would have her passively restrained. I worked closely with the director, set dec, and the actor to find an alternate position – standing, holding onto looped straps on a suspension rig – that allowed the same story to be told within her comfort zone.

Challenges

One of the main challenges of ICing scenes with kink or fetish elements is that they may be written and/or directed by those with a limited knowledge or experience in the subject. Consequently, many, many BDSM scenes and storylines lack authenticity or credibility. Actors who are unfamiliar with some BDSM practices may also need choreography support, especially in using their body to convey power, connection, intention and control (or submission, acceptance, helplessness or exaltation). Often, actors will rely on dialogue or tone to convey these things, but the body and how it holds or cedes space is the more powerful storyteller. It's also important to remember that what drives the symbiotic relationship between a dominant and a submissive is not contempt but consent.

There are plenty of BDSM professionals who can be brought on as consultants to help with a scene's believability. The intimacy coordinator, however, is uniquely positioned to support the actor and production in affirming consent, safety, and comfort.

Resources

The Kink Academy is an excellent place for someone to go for more information on BDSM and kink. There is both free and paid content from experts in a wide variety of formats including podcast, video, blogs articles and more. Many of the presenters are also available for independent consultation.

The following is a list of experienced BDSM practitioners, facilitators and educators, many of whom have also consulted for film, television and theatre or been expert interviews for media content (news, podcasts, print journalism). If you are looking to hire someone local, consider reaching out to one of the practitioners below whose background is similar to what you're looking for and request a referral for a practitioner in your area.

- http://www.loveyourkink.com/ Morgana Maye has a doctorate in clinical psychology and an extensive background in BDSM education. San Francisco, CA.
- https://bondagetherapy.com Elise Graves is a professional bondage practitioner, BDSM content creator and educator. Oakland, CA.
- https://www.mistressnatalie.com/ or https://kinkycoaching.com/ Natalie King is a certified life coach and professional dominatrix with more than 25 years' experience. New York City.
- https://www.yourintimacymuse.com/ Kimberly Ann is an intimacy coach and BDSM facilitator. Los Angeles.
- https://hackinghustling.org/ is a collective of sex workers and allies working at the intersection of technology and social justice issues.
- https://www.eva-oh.com/ Eva Oh is an international BDSM practitioner, educator and podcast host.
- https://www.mistressdamianachi.com Damiana Chi, PhD is a professional dominatrix, BDSM mentor and educator. Los Angeles.
- https://www.mistresstrinitynyc.com/ Trinity is a professional dominatrix specializing in bondage, fetish and the integration of kink and gaming. New York City.
- https://www.kingnoire.com/about-3 King Noire is a Master Fetish Trainer, porn performer and filmmaker, and educator who also lectures on the decolonization of sexuality.

A Conversation with Midori

Brooke M. Haney

> Midori is a multi-hyphenate artist, author and performer. She works as an educator, sexologist and on-set stylist. Perhaps best known for her first of many books, *The Seductive Art of Japanese Bondage*, Midori is largely credited with bringing the eroticism of rope bondage to the English-speaking world. She is an expert in BDSM and kink, particularly femme dominance. She trains therapists in kink fluency and works as a kink expert on fashion, porn and TV/film sets under a plethora of titles she affectionately whittles down to "kink or rope chick." A lot of the ways in which she works are aligned with how intimacy coordinators work, so I had to chat with her.

BROOKE   I know you do a lot of work in fashion, but what is it that is exciting to you about working in TV and film?

MIDORI   Okay, and I do want more work in film and TV because there's a lot of bad out there and I have a lot of experience and perspective that is more practical and humanistic and also with a bigger cultural perspective. Part of my strength is in understanding, being able to work in collaboration with different interests and in what I would call engaging and collaborative consent.

BROOKE   Engaging and collaborative consent is exactly what intimacy coordinating work is all about.

DOI: 10.4324/9781003410553-22

MIDORI	Whether I'm doing collaborative work with other performance artists or other artists, it's about engaged collaborative consent. My strength is in examining how things are done now with a critical eye. Even in how I'm framing terminologies of BDSM, I'm impacting the mental health world with looking at different definitions and looking at terminologies and common assumptions, which is also prevalent in your world with the folks that I've worked with.
BROOKE	Yeah, absolutely. Can we talk a little about rope? A thing that stood out to me in your session at the 2023 Global Majority Intimacy Conference was you advised that, when ICs are working on scenes with rope, they need to recognize the patriarchal hierarchy in rigger culture and ensure that the rope stylist communicates ethically. You said that skills don't equal ethics and expertise can be coercive. For example, a rigger might say, "I know what I'm doing. It's supposed to be uncomfortable." In this case, it is the IC's job to check with the actor to see if the level of discomfort is within their boundaries. Can you tell me more about rope subculture and what you find problematic?
MIDORI	Rope subculture is developing into something really ugly that I just can't stand. Misogyny and Orientalism is getting a pass under respecting tradition, which falls under the whole noble savage. I am also very invested in making sure there aren't dumb things out there about rope and kink.
BROOKE	Can you give me an example of how kink could be better represented?
MIDORI	Yeah, so for example how flogging is presented is very different than say how flogging is taught. Even within the kink subculture, how it's commonly done in presentations, actually doesn't always reflect how people can passionately play.
BROOKE	Ooh, tell me more about that.
MIDORI	So, a typical way that flogging is represented – it's one person braced up against or bound up against something and the person flogging from the back.
BROOKE	Yep.
MIDORI	Why? Why aren't they facing each other? Why isn't flogging in the middle of a good fuck? In a heterosexual model, I could be a guy on my back, with a woman on my cock, and I could be flogging her back. Flogging that I teach, looks a hell of a lot more like an exuberant make out session. People face to face, right? Flogging can be

soft, it can be silly, it can be a short flogger, a long flogger, it can be accompanied more by giggles and moans as well. The complexity of the person topping, their emotional expression is often flattened so badly. I've seen more complex cartoon characters. Facial expressions should be varying, vocal tones should be varying, even if it's a heavy scene of intensity and cruelty.

BROOKE How did we get to these bad and inaccurate examples of kink?

MIDORI What ends up happening, especially lately, self-designated experts are presenting either visually digestible or visually impressive two-dimensional image representation. It becomes an echo chamber of, let's show this complex thing that wows people. Then those who want to be influencers become competitive, and then they end up painting a picture, that that is how people actually kink, which then has a toxic effect of giving people the impression that that's all that is done.

BROOKE As intimacy choreographers, we start with story, right? Can you give some examples of small changes that affect the storytelling?

MIDORI Is the person holding the flog by gripping firmly or gripping awkwardly? Do they grip at the base of the handle or here [the middle]? Do they run their finger through the flogger tail as if they would a loved-one's hair. How a person receiving bondage for the first time might be touching the equipment on their own body.

On set or photo shoots, I've shown people who are performing as topping how to grip and create a little motion, staccato motion, which creates rhythm. Chin up, if you actually want to look competent, if you want to look like a couple of novices, a couple of college kids messing around with bondage, the chin's going to be down. Things like that.

BROOKE In your experience, do the directors really take your input and incorporate it, or do you get pushback?

MIDORI It depends. Now mind you I am not working under any official title other than the kink chick, the rope chick. There was one Canadian indie film that they brought me in and were so good to work with. He had me as a choreographer and took me very seriously. It was a contemporary, magical realist ghost story set in an Asian-Canadian enclave. There's a scene in which the main character is getting bound by magical forces. Instead of rope, I advised him, and he took me up, how about sheer fabric?

BROOKE So beautiful.

MIDORI	Right. So it depends. I'm constantly bumping up against women, and not just me, but other women in the field essentially being dismissed or discredited. Because I teach a lot of soft skills, the interpretation is, "Oh, it's just soft skills, she's not a technical person." (I've only been doing this 30 years.) There is a cultural bias to assuming male folks to be more valid as an expert, not just in our field.
BROOKE	Speaking of being the expert, how do you work with actors or directors who are doing a kink scene for the first time?
MIDORI	If the performer has no experience, I need to show them how to move. And I'm also watching for the stylist work of, "Oh there's a rope out of place. You're holding that crop backward." And then there's the kink culture and Japanese culture being taken seriously, being able to give input on like, "That's not what a love hotel in Japan looks like." Or, "That's a bathrobe, not a kimono. What are you actually trying to say by putting a kimono in this? Because you do know you come off as a racist. Oh, that is what you're trying to do, and that's the bad guy? Got it." There's a lot of things that I'm doing all at once and, depending on what the objective of the work is, I will also go and gather the ropes or the tools as needed.
BROOKE	What are your boundaries around the work you won't take?
MIDORI	Anything that smacks of Orientalism, unless that's something they're trying to satire. Or if the attitude is: "It's just rope. Why do you have to make it so complicated?" Then it's like, no, you don't need me.
BROOKE	Do you have an example of a bondage scene done really well?
MIDORI	*Polite Society*. Oh, you have to see this. It's great. Two South Asian sisters, contemporary London, and it is an over-the-top wedding heist. A South Asian wedding is the central event, so you know, there's all the saris and amazing jewelry. There's a scene in there where the person kidnapped is bound to a chair with sari scarves, and it's done well. And I know that silk is hella strong. The restraint is realistic, because you're in the middle of a wedding, what are you going to capture a person with? It's a brilliant scene. It's a brilliant movie too in the choreography.

Rope Scenes   13

*Megan Gilron and
Brooke M. Haney*

> Megan Gilron comes to their intimacy practice as an advocate and sex educator. She wants everyone to have access to as much pleasure as they can. The media has so much influence over what we think about sex and pleasure and Megan believes that the real sex that people are actually having is so much more interesting than the limited ways that it is portrayed in the media. While I have been practicing rope work occasionally in kink spaces for about ten years, at the time of this writing, I'd only had the opportunity to work on one theatre scene that involved rope. Working on scenes involving rope and bondage is one of Megan's specialties, so I reached out to her to collaborate with me on this chapter.

Note: To specialize in scenes with rope, the IC should have a fair amount of training in rope bondage as a practice. Otherwise, it is essential to have an experienced rigger tie these ties. This chapter contains considerations for "translating" from the real practice to what we are faking for performance. Being honest about your level of expertise is always important as an IC and it is particularly important around scenes that could cause actual physical harm if done incorrectly.

For example, as of the writing of this book, Megan has been tying for five years on and off. Due to the pandemic, there was less opportunity to practice. Only in the last six months of regular practice were they starting to feel confident with simple suspensions, with an experienced model.

Historical and Cultural Considerations

The practice of Shibari and Kinbaku comes from Japanese roots, and rope bondage in general comes from a history of capturing people. The colonization and appropriation of rope play in the English-speaking world, while originally about the act of tying, is often misrepresented as art with a focus on the beautiful visuals that can be created.

"Osada Steve and Hajime Kinoko have broadly the same opinion that 'Shibari' is bondage tying and that Kinbaku is 'Shibari plus emotional connection.'" The tie is for the purpose of the tie, not for the aesthetic. Shibari and Kinbaku are their own version of sex, they don't always need to be combined with an orgasm. Different aspects of rope appeal to different practitioners, the best or most "orgasmic" (in the full-body sense of the word) is sometimes the process of being tied, the subspace state of meditation in rope or the process of being released. These elements are spoken about frequently as being highlights of the practice.

Story

When working on a scene involving rope, we must first consider the story and the characters. Is this a story that is specifically involving Japanese-influenced rope bondage, or is it bondage for the purpose of restraint, for sex? What is the level of experience of the characters? Are they an expert rigger and model or rope top and bottom? Is the rigger an expert, but the bottom is just beginning to experiment? If they are simply using rope for restraint, is it a couple that plays with rope often and we're seeing a bit into the kinky side of their relationship, or is it a couple trying to spice up their sex life by using rope for the first time? Identifying what drives the story and the characters first will inform the rest of the process.

Pre-Production

Establish right away if production will be casting a professional rigger and model who have a relationship or if the scene will be done with actors. In meeting with the producers and director, ask if there is any chance the scene will involve suspension or, if not, what other potential props or sets will be involved in the scene. If there is going to be suspension, can it be faked, or do you need to do a lot of it by pre-rigging in collaboration with the stunt department? It is helpful to get a clear sense of what the shots will be. Knowing the frames will save time. If, for example, we are doing a close up on a shoulder with rope going over it implying a chest harness, and we won't see the tie, we don't need to do the full tie, but rather put the rope on the body with tension.

Ask if seeing the actual ties are necessary for the story, or can we tell it through prep and aftercare? A really interesting scene could simply show the characters before, prepping for the rope scene and then cut to them in aftercare – the top holding the bottom who is covered in rope marks (created by the make-up team).

Actor considerations

- The physics change depending on the weight–height proportion of the person being tied.
- Does the actor playing the rope top have the focus and skill required to tie?
- Does the actor playing the rope bottom have the flexibility and endurance for the scene?
- The IC needs to be aware of the adjustment and prep time that getting in and out of rope will require. In an emergency, one must be able to get an actor out of a tie in less than 30 seconds, so keep safety scissors nearby.
- Have multiple ropes in case the actor/model needs to be cut out.
- Establish safe words. (Green, yellow, red are commonly used in the kink community.) Or, an actor can just communicate by saying they need to be released.

In your actor intake meetings, create expectations. Shape can be described as a yoga position that you have to hold for a long time. If the actor has a piece of nylon, ask them to wrap it around their arm or waist to see how it feels. Let them know what to expect in their body, whether it be the endorphins or a sense of claustrophobia afterwards.

Rope Considerations

- Jute or hemp rope soaks in the body's oils and sweat. It needs to be conditioned, which takes a lot of time, and even after conditioning can feel rough to an actor who is not used to rope.
- Cotton rope is softer, but is a novelty item and should not be used for suspension. Additionally, it can slip, stretch and retract, which can make

it unsafe even for floor work. Under a great deal of tension, be aware of any knots that get too tight to undo easily.
- Bamboo silk rope is naturally anti-bacterial and very soft, but also isn't fit for suspension.
- Consider doing a spot test for allergies and sensitivity – bring one of each option and then buy multiples once you know what you're using.

Preparing for a Rope Scene

- Practice on a model that is the same size as the actor, not only to make sure the choreography is well thought out and will work on the day, but also to get a sense of the timing.
- Let production know how long it takes to get the actor in the ropes and out of the ropes. Determine if it makes sense to get them out during change ups?
- Advocate for rehearsal time at least a week before the scene will be shot. Do a small tie and observe how the actor feels with the rope against their skin. Then, do the full tie. See how long they can stay in it. Run lines to see if it is affecting them cognitively.
- Do tutorials for the actor who has to do the tying on the basic kinds of things a good rigger would know – how to: hold the rope, play with it while looking confident, use the rope to create pleasing friction on the skin, hold the rope bight (midpoint of the rope when folded in half) like a cigarette – the customary way to use Shibari style rope – and how to release the rope.
- Reach out to a consultant if you're stuck – an instructor or other expert in the field.

Choreography Consideration

- The rope is an extension of the character who is the rope top.
- The first thing one usually ties is the hands, to restrain them.
- Texture, tempo and breath are all very valuable ingredients to play with and can be highly motivated by the rope top.
- Frictions are good, because it stays if it's held tight, but once you let go, it falls away.
- Find moments to drop in that add realism. These shout outs to the community will be appreciated.

In Rehearsal

- Pay attention to the temperature of the space, especially if you're outside.
- Ask what feels most sustainable.
- Feet get cold, so socks are helpful for the model.
- Riggers should feel the fingers for numbness – tingle is okay, but if numbness occurs, cut them out.
- Depending on allergies, having fruit and nuts on hand is an excellent tool for keeping an actor's energy strong.
- Finally, encourage the actors to do research. (If you're playing a chef, you will learn to chop vegetables.) Send them resources so that they don't have to start from scratch with a deep dive into the depths of the internet.

Intimacy Kit

Additional items may be needed for your kit when working on scenes involving rope.

- Jojoba oil for treating the ropes.
- Carabiners carry the rope on the kit.
- Cloth for holding the rope.
- Safety scissors.
- Salve for aftercare.
- Ask actors to bring a lotion that works for them, or ask what they prefer and request it from production.

Post-Production

At the end of the shoot day, the IC will check in with the actors and remind the actor who was tied to drink lots of water and avoid foods that cause inflammation. They can offer that an Epsom salt bath may help with stiff or sore muscles. Let the actor know to be aware of their feelings. Even if only tied a bit, in the aftermath, feelings of claustrophobia may come up. If the actor playing the rigger/top was doing anything that implies emotional intensity in the scene, the IC may also recommend intentional closure as the psychosomatic effects of tying or implication of causing harm or pain can be intense for them. The IC may follow up with the actors the next day as well.

Resources

Shibari Study: An online subscription-based tutorial learning platform, it is an effective resource to build up base-level skills considering all safety aspects.

Bibliography

"What Is Shibari and Is It Shibari or Kinbaku?" (2017) *RopeTopia*, July 7, https://rope-topia.com/what-is-shibari-and-is-it-shibari-or-kinbaku/.

A Conversation with Michael Emery

Brooke M. Haney

Michael Emery and I worked together on *Birder*, a queer psychosexual thriller. Despite being a very low budget film, the producers knew that, due to the content, the project needed an intimacy team. Too often, intimacy coordinators have to work alone, and working with a team on this project was a huge blessing. Chelsea Pace did most of the pre-production prep. I came in at the end of prep for the actor meetings with Chelsea and was the lead on-set intimacy coordinator. Leo Monk joined me on set as the assistant intimacy coordinator.

I wanted to talk with Michael, because he was in every scene. In some he wore prosthetics or modesty garments, and in some he was fully nude. The role required simulated pair and group sex as well as violent intimacy. So, we also worked closely with our stunt coordinator, Rob Aronowitz.

BROOKE   One of the reasons you took on this film was because you wanted to challenge yourself. What was it about the challenge that was exciting?

MICHAEL   The character, first of all, wasn't just a straightforward kind of character where he was just a good guy or a bad guy. Christian did things that weren't good or positive, but I felt like he wasn't bad.

BROOKE   It's so important to not judge your character negatively. You can't create a nuanced character from that place.

MICHAEL   I felt like he had a good heart, but he just didn't know how to express his love to people. I grew up with an incredible family, and a mom and dad who loved and supported me throughout my whole life. It's nice to play someone on the flip side. What if you didn't grow up with that love? What if this person was just damaged from Jump Street, and had to figure things out on his own, and that turned me on a lot about the project. Plus, it was so scary what I had to do, so if I'm scared, I'm in.

BROOKE   It's so interesting, because you're talking about being afraid and excited. And I think there's a misconception sometimes that intimacy coordinators are there to make everyone feel comfortable. I believe intimacy coordinators are there to help tell a compelling story and to make sure everyone consents to the way we are telling that story. Sometimes it's consenting to do uncomfortable material. Do you have thoughts on that?

MICHAEL   You saved my life. There were certain times during the shoot where I was just like, oh, I don't know if I can. I mean, one scene in particular, but certain stuff where it was just very, very heavy.

BROOKE   What was most helpful?

MICHAEL   Many things I love about you, but the most important thing is pre-pro. You and Chelsea went through every scene with me that involved some type of intimacy, whether it was just touching a shoulder. You were so meticulous, and it made me feel like, okay, I'm going to be protected here, and I'm going to feel safe here, because you did that with the other actors too. We went through everything before the day started. When we got to set you would huddle all of the other actors around and talk to them about what was going to be done in the scene. Are you okay with this? Are you okay with that? It was just incredible.

BROOKE   The role you played was very physically and mentally challenging. I know you trained physically, to prepare for the running, hiking and swimming, and you had to prepare mentally for the demands of the character. There's also physical preparation that you had to do to discipline your body to be ready for the choreography of the intimate scenes.

MICHAEL   Yes, exactly, exactly. It's like a dance, right? You're dancing with the other person, and it's choreographed. So if you move left, they have to move left, if you move right, they have to move right. And it has to be at a certain subtle pace with the scene because there's dialogue involved too. Your line has to be at a certain point, so they can speak at this point, but there's lots of movement. It's a really integral process and very specific. It's not just alright, let's just lay on our back and let's do it. No, there's tons more that needs to be done. That's why you're there, to direct us in those situations, and you made my life easy, because all I had to do was just concentrate on acting and not worry about anything else.

BROOKE That's the idea, right? You should be focused on the acting. Put all of your energy into that. One of the most difficult scenes in the film was the scene on the island. The material and choreography were challenging for the actors and the location was challenging for the crew. We could only get to the island by boat, and the boat's motor exploded that morning. So, the scene got pushed to the end of the day, and we were fighting the light. It was already going to be tricky, and we set up a bunch of protocols in advance, but then on the day we had to pivot. I didn't feel we actually had enough time to fully rehearse everything. So, I opted to talk you and the other two actors through the choreography as we shot it.

MICHAEL It actually worked well for me, because it was toward the end of the shoot, and I was dreading the day. It was pushed so far that it gave me mentally more time to prep. Once we got to that scene, even though it wasn't easy, I was more mentally ready. It was a testament to you, because you guided me through that scene. That would have been very very difficult if you weren't there for support and guidance.

BROOKE That's a really tricky thing, because it's really easy for time to become coercive. We all knew that the next day was our last day of shooting. We knew we needed this scene. For me it felt like a really fine balance between taking care of the film and making sure to take care of the actors.

One thing that really helped was after the first take, you communicated with me. You said, "I've got one more left in me." And I said that to Nate – we only have one more.

MICHAEL I gave everything, I did. I emptied the tank that last take.

BROOKE Afterwards, you got light headed and nearly fainted.

MICHAEL Yeah, Josh (Friedman), the amazing AD caught me and he was like, "Take a knee."

BROOKE I sent over Sara Walsh, our medic, and she brought water and checked you out while I checked in with the other actors. Why do you think you hyperventilated?

MICHAEL I just wasn't breathing. I was so in the moment. I was trying to push through fear. I was trying to get to the finish line in the best way I could, because I was so scared to do it. And actually, there was excitement too like I'm in it. This is it. We're doing it. So I stood up too fast. And then I didn't take enough air in and then that kind of happened. But it's such a beautiful scene, though. It's incredible.

BROOKE That's an important thing for actors to know, working on intimacy or anything really emotionally charged, remember to breathe. Also, know how much you have to give and communicate it so that the filmmakers can make sure they get their shots without asking the actors to do more than they can safely.

MICHAEL Right. Exactly. Exactly. Your body can react differently to super dark emotional scenes. Whether you're crying, you're laughing or you're screaming it's just, you have to listen to your body and know where you can go emotionally.

BROOKE At the end of the day, is there anything you do for closure when you're working on a role that's this difficult?

MICHAEL I like to stretch. I do lots of stretching, meditations. I listen to some really calming music, and it brings me back down. I can go up really high, but then getting back down to a normal level is so important for your mental state and physical state.

BROOKE Absolutely. Unfortunately, the industry has glamorized actors that go so deep they get stuck in the role. It romanticizes that sometimes, but you were able to be 100 percent there when you were working, and then you let it go.

MICHAEL Yeah, I mean, I struggle with it still sometimes too. I'll break down and cry after I get back to my hotel. But then I just take a shower, and I listen to music and come back to baseline, you know, which is what you need to do. It just seems exhausting to me to be at level 10 all the time, you know? Because then you have nothing to give the next day.

BROOKE Exactly. You as the actor have to teach your body that it can trust you to know your limits and communicate them.

Stories of Trauma   14

Brooke M. Haney

> Content Note: Suicide is discussed and described. Other traumatic events are simply mentioned.

There are many possible types of scenes that involve trauma; intimate partner violence, medical trauma or death, micro aggressions or aggressions and death by suicide are a few examples. In this chapter, I focus on the types of things that may be expected of an intimacy professional when working on scenes that portray or discuss trauma. To be clear, I am not talking about working with actors/directors/crew on their personal trauma, as that is outside the scope of practice of an IC. In the next chapter, Amy Northup will delve into sexual assault and non-consent to give a more detailed analysis of one of the more common kinds of trauma on which IPs work.

> If you are someone who has experienced trauma and are considering working on projects that reflect that trauma, remember that it is your responsibility to decide if you are currently healthy enough to work on that subject. Suffering and self-harm for your art is not heroic or romantic, it is unsafe for you and for those with whom you may be working. While there are, of course, things we won't anticipate that may activate us, a prepared artist will have disciplined practices around self-care and a support network outside of the project.

Trauma On Screen or Off

Characters may experience trauma on stage or screen. For example, in the short film *She's Clean*, by Jenn Harris, a character, dealing with their PTSD, when triggered, turns from romantic to violent. Alternatively, a scene or project may involve characters dealing with a trauma that they have experienced in the past (off-screen), as in *New Lives*, by Joey Schwitzer, where two characters, living in Brooklyn, rediscover romantic intimacy after having escaped Nazi concentration camps in World War Two. When dealing with scenes of trauma, there are several ways in which intimacy professionals can support the production.

The Team

It is important to be clear that the work of intimacy professionals is not to make folks feel "comfortable." That can lead to the wrong assumptions about our role on set or in rehearsal. Many roles that an actor may take on will be uncomfortable. As long as actor's boundaries are given space to be expressed and respected, actors can mindfully do this kind of brave work. Making known the scope of practice for an IC and their team early on will help bring clarity to all who are collaborating. And when things come up later in the process, and they often do, keep clear boundaries around your job and help by making recommendations for additional folks or resources that may need to be considered.

There is an argument (see Chapter 5, "Mental Health Coordinators") that scenes of trauma are often not in the scope of practice for an IC, that they fall more in line with what mental health coordinators do. Afterall, IC work is usually defined as scenes involving nudity, hyper exposure and simulated sex, or other kinds of physical intimacy. This is why I have included scenes of trauma in this book as a specialty rather than a competency. For those of us who do work regularly on scenes of trauma, we do so acknowledging that intimacy can be more than just physical, it can involve emotional vulnerability as well.

That said, having a mental health coordinator or psychologist as part of the team may also be wise. Even with the best intentions and practices around self-care, there are bound to be folks involved who have a connection to the trauma and something may come up. Having a qualified professional who can watch for and help with this can save time and protect your team and the project.

Depending on the type of trauma being portrayed or discussed and your or the director's level of expertise on the subject, calling in a consultant who specializes in the content might also be beneficial. They can also be helpful with the dramaturgy and research.

Fight directors (theatre) or stunt coordinators (film/TV) are perhaps the most common collaborators we work with on these types of scenes (see Chapter 4, "Intimacy and Violence"). Discussing and exploring the possibilities for the scene will help to determine how you will choreograph together and who will take the lead. This is imperative for a smooth process.

If the trauma is racial in nature or aimed at another marginalized group, and you are not well versed or do not have lived experience in that area, consider working with a cultural consultant. When working on scenes involving trauma, intensive dramaturgical research to understand the issues of the show is incredibly important for accurate and respectful storytelling.

Language and Research

Be accurate in your depictions of the trauma and in the ways you talk about it. "Trigger" is a word that has been overused. When we do this, it loses its specificity. Trigger in our lexicon has started to mean anything that upsets someone or makes them think of a negative experience in the past. However, a true emotional or mental health trigger is something that activates one's fight, flight, freeze or fawn response. It is often accompanied by increased adrenaline, raised heartbeat, sweating, difficulty breathing, intense emotion and avoidant behavior (yes, these are choreographic clues). When working on a scene of trauma, it is imperative to use trigger accurately as it may be a catalyst for a particular action or moment of storytelling.

Much like we desexualize language when choreographing intimacy, deload your language around the trauma (including how the scene is named or described on the callsheet), and be aware of the meaning behind your words. For example, there are various ways people refer to suicide and implications behind each. When we say someone "committed suicide," we are invoking a religious bent – committing a sin, committing a crime. When we say "died by suicide," we are implying an understanding of some mental health conditions, depression for example, as a disease that isn't survived. And both of these two examples are very Eurocentric. Not everyone (even in the West) views suicide as a negative. Some folks, who don't view their birth as a requirement to continue life, see it as a viable option. According to Adam Acar, "**Seppuku is honorable death** or ritualistic suicide by disembowelment that can only be conducted by a samurai." And, even within this act, whether you call it Seppuku or Hara-kiri (often used in the West) denotes a different point of view. "Japanese people almost never use the word harakiri and prefer the word **seppuku** instead. Harakiri refers to the action of cutting stomach while seppuku represents the ritual and the traditional procedure of cutting the stomach" (Maikoya, 2022). Doing the research on the trauma you are portraying or discussing is incredibly important. How you talk about your project is important, how your characters talk about their experience can be very informative.

Actor Considerations

In your actor intake meetings, much like you wouldn't assume anything about someone's sexual experience or ask for that disclosure, don't make assumptions about their relationship to trauma. While most of us are empathetic, we aren't therapists. These meetings are meant to prepare the actors for the work on the day, not to give us insight into their lives. Instead, use trauma informed practices. Give lots of information, so that they know what to expect. Empower them by asking what they need as far as support in order to do their best work on set. Eliminating surprises as much as possible is a great way to minimize possible harm.

Of course there will be times that an actor (or someone else on the production team) may disclose to you. Remember that you can have boundaries around that disclosure. If you are comfortable hearing it, thank them for sharing and bring the conversation back to the work. Ask how they anticipate the information will affect them on the day, what support they have already set up for themselves, and what ways you can support them within the bounds of an IC's job.

On Set

Even if there isn't nudity, hyper exposure or sexual actions, consider closing the set or at least limiting the number of folks in the room. The intensity of the work required for the actor should be respected, and limiting the number of folks in the space often is helpful around concentration or focus. Remember to have your closed set memo included with the call sheet.

Encourage fewer takes and frequent breaks; the body doesn't know it's fake. When we put our body in positions of fear, grief, terror, etc., the body experiences it as if it is really happening. Allowing actors to mark in rehearsals and letting them know when their face is out of frame can be helpful in allowing them to sustain their energy for the shots that really need it.

Make sure to check in as needed with the actors playing victim and aggressor. Both roles are difficult.

Offer Closure Tools

There are a variety of closure practices that have developed over the years that take anywhere from one to 20 minutes, depending on what the actor needs.

While intimacy choreographers are not mental health professionals, we can work in collaboration with them. The closure tools we have can be very effective for actors to use in addition to their own self-care. Closure is an important skill for actors to work on themselves, and an intimacy choreographer can help facilitate the learning when appropriate, as well as make space and time for it in a production.

For some actors, putting on and taking off their costume serves as the container to their work. Some breathe their character out as a color. There are an infinite number of possible ways for actors to create closure for themselves. *Staging Sex* has a version of de-roling that allows actors to clearly articulate the separation between their work and themselves. Tapping in/out, originally taught to me by Judi Lewis Ockler, who learned it from Intimacy Directors International, has become a very popular way to create a very clear beginning and end to the work of the scene.

When the actor's actual body is in fight/flight/freeze/fawn, adrenaline is pumping, the heart beats at over 100 beats per minute and the blood pressure rises, it can take about 20 minutes or more for the body to regulate (Gottman and Silver, 1999). For these situations, *The Actor's Warm Down* is a 20-minute practice I developed that involves breath and sound work, yoga, meditation, power poses and a dance party. The aim is to remind your body that you are safe, that you can open up and have agency in the physical positions you choose to put it.

For the actors reading this book, I encourage you to experiment with what works best for you. Consider it a skill like your voice or movement training. An actor who knows and can articulate their boundaries, who has a disciplined body and who has invested time in establishing closure practices that works for them is one that is ready to do this kind of work.

Self-Care

As the intimacy coordinator, you may need to do your own closure work on these types of scenes. Plan time for that. Be sure to set clear expectations and boundaries around your availability post shoot or production. Being prepared with resources to offer can help to maintain your boundaries and keep you within your scope of practice.

Audience Consent

In film and TV, content advisories are pretty standard. From the vague: "The following is only intended for mature audiences. Viewer discretion is advised." To the slightly more detailed: "RATED TV-MA language, drug use, self-harm, violence."

It's much more common to be asked to help create the content notice, in a theatre production, though including one on a call sheet can be helpful to keep the crew apprised of what to expect each day. When creating a consent advisory, ask yourself: what are the opportunities I have to give my audience agency to opt into the show?

Consider both the content the play deals with directly.

- Example: *She Kills Monsters* explores themes of grief, suicide, violence, homophobia and sexuality.

And also possible microaggressions or aggressions that come up in the dialogue or character descriptions.

- Example: *She Kills Monsters* also contains strong language and fatphobia.

The pushback I most often get around content notices is when a company is concerned about spoilers. Consider having a sign in the lobby that says something like: "Content advisory for this show can be found on page eight of the program and may contain spoilers." When marketing the show on the theatre's website, create a link, "Click here for the content advisory for this production." Then, your audience even gets agency over whether they want to read your content advisory or not. Offer a place folks can go for more information. For example, if your content advisory is graphic violence, an audience member might wonder what kind of violence. By giving them a place to ask further questions, you not only keep from giving too much away, you also give them the opportunity to inquire about their individual needs.

Resources

The Embodiment Institute has initiatives, courses, a speaker series and resources all aimed at changing the conversation, practice and politics of healing.

Bibliography

Andrews, Evan. (2016) "What Is Seppuku?" *History.com*, January 11, https://www.history.com/news/what-is-seppuku.

Gottman, John and Nan Silver. (1999) *Seven Principles for Making Marriage Work*, Orion Spring.

Maikoya. (2022) "Seppuku and Harakiri Explained: Facts and Differences." *Tea Ceremony Japan Experiences MAIKOYA*, February 13, https://mai-ko.com/travel/japanese-history/samurai/harakiri-and-suppuku/.

A Conversation with Amnon Lourie and Nate Dushku

Brooke M. Haney

> Amnon Laurie is the writer and Nate Dushku the director of *Birder*. I was super stoked to serve on the intimacy team for this project with Chelsea Pace and Leo Monk. Realistic representation in queer stories is one of the things that brings me the most joy in this profession. If I could tell these kinds of stories every day for the rest of my life, I'd be incredibly fulfilled.

Content Note: Mention and description of childhood sexual assault.

BROOKE   When we first started talking about *Birder*, you said that one of your priorities was an accurate and realistic representation of queer sex. Why was that important?

NATE   I think that there's not a lot of that out there. I remember, you know, growing up, I think it was just like a soap opera or *Beverly* or *Melrose Place* or something, where the first time I saw a kiss on camera, it was literally like, they leaned in, and then it was very 1980s, the blinds closed, and there was like a shadow of it. I mean, we've come a long way from just a kiss and silhouette. You know now I still think they cut away. And even with hetero sex, they cut away a lot, but especially with queer sex and their films in which you do get that, they almost feel like they get relegated to the soft

	core LGBTQ section at the bottom of Netflix or something, you just don't really see a lot of it.
AMI	I think for me, Nate and I are aligned on a lot, for obvious reasons. We've been married now for 18 years, and a lot of our sex life is shared, I would say 95 percent of our sex life is shared. Yeah. When I was nine years old, I was molested by a family friend, and I'm a survivor of sexual assault. And it was an interesting thing for me growing up and dealing with that, because it was an 18-year-old person having sexual relations with a nine-year-old. It wasn't the kind of thing where it was like, I was forced into it physically or even manipulated into it. A homosexual 18-year-old boy posed the "suck my dick" question, kind of jokingly, and I, as a nine-year-old, was like, yeah, sure. And so dealing with the trauma that as you grow up it becomes a part of your sexual health, it becomes a part of the world that you live in, and so much of being gay and queer and sexually marginal in this society is taking these weird and traumatic and, like, not necessarily dealt with experiences and kind of conforming them into your adult life. A lot of adult queer sexuality is that, unafraid of living in these marginal places where BDSM and fetish and kink is a fundamental part. So in our film, we're dealing with trauma. And we're dealing with this coercive unempathetic drama. And if we're gonna do it right, we've got one shot. And it was important for us to find someone who would help us articulate that trauma without making it a vector for the trauma, but more like an observation of it.
BROOKE	So that's why you brought in an intimacy team?
AMI	We didn't want to hurt anyone, but we also wanted to tell the truth, like, we live in a weird fucking world, and our sex is a representation of that. It's a representation of our traumas, and being marginal, and queer sexuality is very much that. We need to say it right, otherwise people won't get the message.
BROOKE	For a feature film, this was a relatively small budget.
NATE	Tiny.
BROOKE	And even though SAG/AFTRA doesn't require intimacy coordinators, they're recommended, you planned to hire an IC from the start despite it being a big decision financially. What was it about working with an IC that was so important to you?
NATE	I think, going back to what was talked about – the real representation of queer sex – dealing with trauma, dealing with kink, types of sex that are often shamed or looked away from and, like, we got immediately kicked off on a casting website, and then a lot

	of people just passed right away, knowing very little about the film, or reading certain passages and just kind of going, no, this is too much, or it's crossing the line. So you know that you're gonna have an uphill battle. So we just thought, we've got to do this with an intimacy coordinator, because if we don't have one, it's going to be so much harder to gain people's trust. As simple as that, and frankly, it started to work right away. The second we told people that we had an intimacy coordinator, more people are willing to talk, their ears are a little bit more open, you know?
AMI	I think on a very fundamental level, that's for business, you need to say this is the standard to which I hold myself. For me, one of the things that was really important is we want people to be able to regard this kind of trauma, this unempathetic, psychopathological force, which does damage to queer people and marginal people, but we don't want to visit that trauma on anyone in the making of this.
BROOKE	Right, because of the scarcity of work in the industry, actors are so hungry for work, especially unique work, that it can be easy to take advantage.
AMI	It's really easy as an artist, to say it's really hard to make art. So I'll do whatever it takes. And that can cause people to walk away with damage. And it was really important to us that the film served as a vehicle for us not only to explore our own trauma and find catharsis, but for the people that were a part of it, to be able to regard it and experience it, and maybe hold space for it, without having to walk away with a little piece of it. Because there's nothing worse in this world, whether it's this business or any other when someone gets damaged, and then passes it on down the line, because that's the cycle that we're trying to speak out against in the movie.
NATE	You know, I come from the New York theatre world, I used to be a performer. So I've been in situations that were really uncomfortable. And also have a lot of experiences around people that work in TV and film. And, you know, just knew there was a better way. And so with the popularity of intimacy coordinators growing, something that we really wanted to do was to try to just create a safer space. Simple as that.
AMI	It's really easy to say you mean well, but the best way to mean well is to spend the money.
BROOKE	I appreciate that you say safer space. It's not possible to create a fully safe space and we need to admit that. My job is to create a

	safer space, a brave space where actors can feel free to bring their whole selves to what may be very uncomfortable material.
NATE	In the first few weeks, soaking up all the information that we're getting off of you and even people that were interviewed that didn't get put on, learning the language. Right away it became very clear like, yes, this feels good. This is right. We're doing this for the right reasons.
AMI	Also, we're fucking old. For the creative arts, you know, we're in our forties. And it's different, we're not old in the sense like you can write really well, you can direct or produce whatever. But there's like this currency in the way young people, the new generation, thinks about identity and the way people and identity come into contact with each other. You need a professional to help you key into that currency so that when you do talk to people, it's direct and it's clear.
BROOKE	You didn't just hire me, you basically hired a team. Chelsea did most of the prep. And to your point about age, I'm also in my forties. But Leo…
AMI	Everyone's favorite person in the entire world!
BROOKE	Yeah. Leo had that younger vibe and had so much knowledge, and was such an asset to the team, with their thoughts, with choreography, coordinating the background actors, really everything.
AMI	Yeah, we're all smart and fun and kind and fresh and whatever. But there's just this central weight to being able to speak the language that everybody is going to key into. And for me, the role of intimacy coordination in the film that we did was be that communication hub, so that every time a very important communication that required intimacy to be involved went through, it was filtered without damage.
BROOKE	Ami, you write your intimacy very explicitly. Sometimes when I get a script, it'll say like, "They kiss," or, "They share a passionate moment." The way you write really walks us through the details, giving us the ability to picture what's happening. Why is that how you write?
AMI	Well, I would say I'm very lucky to have a very talented partner, who, when I do write for us, it's a conversation.
BROOKE	You're communicating to Nate how you picture it happening.
AMI	And one of the reasons that we write so explicitly, is because we want people to know that we're not ashamed of the action itself. We're not asking someone to do something disgraceful. We're

	asking someone to take on something that might be difficult to conceive of if they've never conceived of it before. But we want to be clear, because clarity is kindness.
BROOKE	And it allowed people to opt in.
AMI	That's literally, if someone says yes, they're saying yes to your vision, they're not saying yes just to an idea. They're saying, oh, okay, I see that. And I understand what's expected. Dangerous sex is sexy to a lot of people, kind of one of the most sexy things in sex is like getting close to someone's end. But yeah, I think it's important to let people see how it really is out there. You do have to prepare someone's asshole or anus before you stick a dick in it, you usually use your mouth or a lot of lube. And it's like this is what sex is, it's procedural. And hopefully you figure out how to make your procedural stuff feel sexy and then you get really good at sex.
BROOKE	Most queer folks didn't get an education from our parents, most of us were raised straight, most of us were raised cis. We didn't get queer sex in our sex education classes in school, so any representation is precious, because it's part of our education.
AMI	And we owe it to ourselves to be honest, and non-judgmental.
BROOKE	Nate, what do you see as the relationship between director and IC?
NATE	Well, you helped me with that, because we interviewed quite a few people, and everybody kind of approaches it differently. Directors approach it differently, ICs approached it differently. And, you know, I learned a lot. Certain intimacy coordinators read our script, and decided ahead of time that what was required of the actors and the story didn't feel safe to them. You came in and said, I see the vision behind the script, and I'm here to help with this vision. So once we had that alignment, I think we were then looking for actors that could join us in telling the story. So I think the IC and director are, yes, aligned to keep the talent safe, but also aligned to tell the story.

And I think a big thing for me is learning from you, and then learning how to, you know, adapt the way I talk and adapt the way a set works. Oftentimes, and I don't think all directors do this, but I felt really comfortable giving the set over to you. Almost like giving it to a choreographer, or a stunt coordinator, and then watching you work with the actors. |
| AMI | But isn't that like you get to watch that interaction between your intimacy coordinator and your actors, and then you learn about |

	your actors and what you're doing on set, you're both storytellers essentially.
BROOKE	This story was very important to me. It thrilled me actually. And, it was a very special set to be on, because a significant majority of the folks on set were queer. I wanted to make sure we took care of our community while we told our story.
NATE	You know, I think that this idea that somebody can change their mind during production was always scary to me, because you kind of feel like, well, they signed up for this. So, hopefully, they're gonna give us what they signed up for.
BROOKE	And we did have an actor change their boundaries at one point, and we were able to reframe the shot and keep telling the story.
NATE	These days of beating a performance out of somebody, it's just not the world we live in anymore. You hear about these great directors of the past, but it's just not the way I work, even though I know it exists out there.
AMI	We do have one shot every time you tell a story and we're telling a very dark queer story. We call our movie a psychosexual, queer tragedy. That is the genre, it's a tragedy, there's a very dark, hard stop, and it is definitely a queer movie. And if we didn't do it right, across the board, at every point, if we did do something wrong, it would not be good for just us, we would be holding the line for a lot of other people and other storytellers. And it's important to represent your culture, on the stage, the public stage, with as much respect and honor that you would want for yourself as a queer person as everyone else.

15

Non-consent and Sexual Violence

Amy Northup

> Amy Northup is an expert in the field of staging sexual assault (SA), sexual violence (SV) and non-consent (NC). Beyond her work as an intimacy coordinator, Amy is a trained Crisis Counselor with The Crime Victims Treatment Center in New York City where she provides crisis counseling, emotional support and advocacy to survivors of sexual assault and intimate-partner violence. She is also a longtime trainer with OutSmartNYC, a non-profit dedicated to sexual violence prevention in nightlife and hospitality spaces. As a result of these additional layers of training and expertise, she is uniquely positioned to talk about staging this kind of work, and has an expanded scope of practice that may not apply to all practitioners. There are some skills that Amy has, where another IC might want to bring in additional support from a mental health coordinator or therapist.

Content Note: This chapter will discuss approaching scenes of sexual violence and rape. While there are no explicit depictions, we do discuss examples of scenarios an IC may need to navigate, and examples from the author's experience. Please take care while reading, and move through this chapter at a speed that is safe for you to do so.

First thing's first – what IS sexual violence?

While sometimes a script will come to you that clearly depicts sexual violence or assault, others may be less clear. As is often the case with sexual violence, it can be less cut and dry than we'd like it to be.

Like it or not, the media has conditioned the way we define sexual violence, who experiences it and who is capable of perpetrating it. You know the formula: our victim is a young, thin, cis, white woman; the perpetrators are always men, and often men of color. State-to-state legal definitions of rape and sexual assault vary, but we reduce the complexity of the range of experiences when we minimize it to the unwanted penetration of a penis into a vagina.

The actual spectrum of sexual violence – and who experiences it – is much more encompassing. People of all identities can experience – and perpetrate – violence and harm. More often than not, the perpetrator is someone close to the survivor, not a stranger lurking in the shadows. When we move away from a heterosexual and penetrative definition of assault, we further expand our understanding of sexual violence to be any non-consensual sexualized verbal, emotional, physical contact, abuse or harassment. Consider also scenes of stalking, gender-based violence, online harassment, intimate partner and domestic violence, workplace harassment – the list is expansive. For the purposes of this work, I encourage you to think broadly – and intersectionally – about the umbrella term of sexual violence, and determining if a project includes any elements of non-consent.

> The term intersectionality was first introduced in 1989 by critical race theorist Kimberlé Crenshaw. The term, notably and unsurprisingly, has gone through a buzzwordification that threatens to dilute its original intention and impact. In her own words, "intersectionality can get used as a blanket term to mean, 'Well, it's complicated.' Sometimes, 'It's complicated' is an excuse not to do anything."
> https://www.law.columbia.edu/news/archive/kimberle-crenshaw-intersectionality-more-two-decades-later
>
> I encourage the reader to join me in the ongoing work of deepening our understanding and practice of terms and movements like this – the work of Black women and femmes that have been co-opted and bastardized – and hold ourselves to high integrity in how we implement them in our work.

Sexual violence shows up in our storytelling in a few ways: in some, the story is rooted in and about the SA; others, the story is happening AND so does sexual violence; or – and this we seek to avoid – none of the creators intended to depict SV, but are disguising SV as romance.

Even if I'm working on a scene that isn't explicitly **about** sexual violence, I will often ask a director how they envision consent in the scene. This normalizes consent considerations in ALL scenes, and opens the door to saturating consensual scenes with more accurate and nuanced depictions of consent practices. We can get into really juicy choreographic beats of non-verbal consent, or add subtle moments of dialogue (hint: dirty talk can be consent work, y'all!) – all while avoiding making the whole thing feel like an after-school special. If I have flagged beats that may potentially read as non-consensual and discover that wasn't the intention, we can make adjustments. If the director understands that consent is complicated and that, in a single sexual encounter, individual experiences may differ, we can add layers of behavioral nuance to complicate.

> Example conversation with a director: "Let's chat about this choking moment! I know you said it is important to the story that this be a *fully consensual* interaction – instead of having Character A directly place their hands around Character B's throat, how would you feel about adding a beat of A placing a bit of pressure with an open palm on the collar bone, then have Character B grab A's wrist and move the hand tightly around their own neck?"

Not only have we added a (much needed) depiction of non-verbal consent – I'll argue we're also getting a much steamier scene. And, we're letting the receiver of a potentially risky action control it – a standard approach to safety in stunt work.

Once you are clear with the director that you are *intentionally* telling a story of SV/NC, it's crucial to ensure everyone is on the same page. We want to avoid discovering in a rehearsal room that we have different understandings of what consent – or lack thereof – is happening in the scene. Having one person in the room reading an act as non-consensual while another is speaking of it as consensual can deeply mirror the survivor experience, and be incredibly triggering.

It's important to tease this out in your initial one-on-one conversations, and not in a group setting. This allows any teaching moments to be handled deftly and with grace, and avoid them being harmful to others. Be prepared to meet people where they are, without attacking, condescending or judging.

Much of the pushback around intimacy coordination is rooted in fear. This conversation requires an incredible amount of nuance, but – in an attempt to put it succinctly – we are, of course, associated with the #metoo movement (please see above note about intersectionality – #metoo is a movement that was started by Tarana Burke a decade before it went viral in Hollywood). It is not uncommon for folks to assume our presence in a room indicates there is already a problem, or that we are there to punish or condemn. Gently, I invite us to recognize that yes, there are predators among us. But more commonly, we are ALL capable of causing harm, and so often do not intend to do so. While keeping impact centered, we can also make space for intention. I hold strongly to the value that in order for us to be culture changers, we need to be people whom it is safe to make mistakes around – people that can almost educate without anyone knowing it even happened, because we don't weaponize shame. *Doing this privately can turn the volume down on the shame of someone who has mis-stepped, while buffering the harm for the person that may have received it had they been in the room. Again, this does not always apply and must be considered with great nuance.*

General Considerations

- Survivors are everywhere, and hold all identities; be mindful of who you may be viewing as "more likely" to need support. I see this often, for example, in people assuming that cis men in the room haven't experienced sexual violence, so may not instinctually check in with them at the same level they would a cis woman.
- Remember that the actors performing the scenes aren't the only ones interacting with the content; you may be working with a director that has written a very personal story. Crew members may find repeated exposure to the scene difficult. Work with your AD teams to ensure that folks have access to scripts as ahead of time as possible, and encourage the inclusion of content considerations and therapeutic resources on call sheets and in safety meetings.
- I find it helpful to avoid preciousness in this work in general, but particularly when approaching scenes of trauma. This may seem a bit counter intuitive, but coddling or walking on eggshells can in and of itself load a trigger. This is admittedly a fine line, and as always – *meet people where they are.*
- Remain consistent about desexualizing your language **without talking around and invalidating what the scene is about.** Instead of, "We have a

scene coming up today with... you know... some not nice things happening..." opt for, "Tomorrow's work includes a scene depicting sexual assault. Please take care of yourselves and each other, and let us know if you need a break from the room or any support during or after." Keep this quick, keep the tone fairly neutral and kind – name the thing honestly, without loading it or infusing it – and go about the work.

- Remember you *cannot "do consent" for other people*. Survivors of sexual violence have endured being stripped of their autonomy. Whether someone is coming with a history of trauma or experiencing it in the moment, overbearing "help" can feel like further having agency taken away from them. Never take action on an actor's behalf without explicit permission or request from them to do so (this applies to ALL scenes, not just those of SV/NC). If something goes wrong, validate that it happened, ask how they are, check in with them about what they'd like to do next. Always let them take the lead, and trust that even if you don't agree with their decision, *they know best what it is they need*.

  Instead, in every micro moment, every interaction – how are you expanding their **access** to their own choice? How are you making their "no" or "maybe" or "can we take a quick break" a little easier to reach out and grab for themselves?

- Similarly, trauma responses and support look different for everyone. Some people are going to want extra levity and jokes; others need more quiet and space. Others still will respond to you being very present and caretaking. Don't force an energy YOU think makes sense on the work. Consent in all things.

- As ever, be mindful of the coercive nature of urgency. Our job is to add space and time to someone receiving information and having to respond to it.

- A core tenant of my work across the board, but specifically in this specialty, is from adrienne maree brown's *Emergent Strategy*; to *move at the speed of trust*.

- When it comes to working with the actors specifically, it can be tempting to focus your support on those whose characters are experiencing violence – but it can also be incredibly difficult to embody a perpetrator. Naming that to the performers doing so can be empowering for them in feeling valid in the need for support. Folks can be so aware of how difficult it may be for their scene partner they forget to take care of themselves.

- If the scene is particularly physically violent, it is likely that there will be stunt doubles. While they may be more accustomed to technically

executing this work, I have always found them wildly appreciative when they are given the opportunity to check in beforehand and throughout about any additional needs they may have, wardrobe details, etc. And of course, in this case the stunt coordinator should be handling the choreography.
- Consider too that non-consent in scripts is not always expressed physically. Check in with actors about any language boundaries they may have for improv or even scripted dialogue (i.e., *"Slut is actually really off the table for me, and it's currently scripted. Can we ask the director if 'bitch' or 'whore' could be an alternative here, and still tell the story?"*).

Working with Actors

When doing prep calls, start with open-ended and general questions to warm up into the convo. Avoid things like "how are you feeling about this rape scene?". Try instead: "Any initial thoughts or responses to the scene you wanna start with?"

When you do begin to speak to the sexual violence in the scene, *never* ask if someone has a history of trauma that you should be aware of. You'll move through the work the same way regardless, with all parties. Name what the scene is before discussing choreography or asking about red/yellow/green areas, and remind them that their boundaries never need to be justified.

That said – be prepared for disclosures of personal experience, and to receive them in a supportive but neutral way – validate while avoiding escalating reactions (shock, anger, coddling, etc.). An example of response to disclosure might be:

> *"Thank you for sharing that with me, and trusting me with that. I know that could inform how you're feeling on the day as you work on this, so let's talk about what kind of container we can create together to make working on this as safe as possible for you. Is there anything in particular in this scene that stands out to you that you may want to adjust?"*

Notice here that we don't ask for further or specific details of personal experience. This isn't about being cold or uncaring; it's demonstrating that they do not need to lay their trauma out in order to be believed and supported, or in order for their boundaries to be respected.

If an actor has disclosed to you, never share that disclosure with others when sharing requests for accommodation or adjustment, unless the actor has explicitly asked you to let others know.

Actors want to give themselves generously to their characters, and it is not uncommon for someone to *want* to use something they know will be triggering to them. I think it's important here to differentiate the difference between **activating their system (uncomfortable)** and **triggering it (unsafe)**. The latter is unpredictable and unrepeatable, as well as dangerous. A trigger may move the nervous system into hyper or hypo-arousal, to the point of rendering the actor no longer present and responsive in the scene or to their own bodies and signals. Staying activated within their window of tolerance allows them to continue to give generously to their character's emotional life while staying present and responsive to the world around them – and THAT'S where great performances happen.

Remind them that they are great <u>actors</u> – self-harm in the name of their art is not an option.

Work with your actor to create a "safety plan" for if a trigger does occur. Avoiding the topic of trigger or talking about it as a thing to be avoided at all costs can add to the feeling of panic or shame if it does happen. Having a safety plan can make it actually less likely to happen and strip it of its power, not to mention make it much more manageable if it does – because you've got a plan.

Think of a safety plan as a map:

If _____ happens, then I'm going to do _____, _____ or _____. I might need you to _____. Please don't _____. It helps me when _____.

Particularly in these scenes, use character names as opposed to actor names when reviewing choreography options. (Adam is pushed up against the wall – NOT "YOU are pushed up against the wall..."). This models for performers finding space between themselves and their characters. This "container" work is, of course, also a closure practice, which becomes particularly important with scenes of SV/NC. Planning them ahead of time is safety planning. Creating a game plan for closure with the artist allows them to go safely into the work knowing there is a solid plan for coming out of it. This isn't limited to closure directly after the scene; I'll also often talk through what the actor will do when they get home, and in the days following. (i.e., take a bath or watch a favorite show, make an appointment with their therapist or plans with a friend the day after the shoot.)

In addition to encouraging actors to think through their own self and community care plans, I personally keep some additional tools for nervous system regulation in my kit – fidget toys, ice and heating packs, weighted items, noise reducing ear plugs, bubbles, etc. That said, putting as much of an actor's self-care in their own hands is ideal. You can ask if there are any "creature comforts" an actor likes to have on hand.

> On scope of practice: In several places here, I'm speaking to ways that I include somatic nervous system regulation in my approach to these scenes, which I personally feel comfortable doing because of additional training outside of IC training. While all ICs should have crisis response skills, remember that we are not therapists, and keeping a clear scope of practice is healthiest for everyone involved. It's crucial to not over promise what you can do and what your skillset is. Have referrals to local resources ready if someone needs continued support beyond the day. Passing a scene to someone with this specialty, or bringing in a mental health coordinator to work in tandem with you is a powerful choice, not a weakness.

On Set

When shooting the scene, I work with the director to let performers know when possible if certain frames don't require seeing their face or certain parts of the body, so they can mark on those ones. There's absolutely no reason to be putting yourself fully through the trauma of a scene if we're not seeing the work you're doing on a particular set up. When possible, limit the number of takes and adjust masking as you go to get only what is needed for that shot. I often find actors worry if they're not triggered ENOUGH they feel they aren't going deep enough. Container/anchor work is about doing just that. It's *great* if they're not 100 percent connected; that is what their body is built to do, and it's serving them.

Final thoughts

This work isn't formulaic, the only best practice is that there are no best practices. Some of these thoughts may be entirely wrong or ill-fitting for your particular combination of circumstances or the humans you're working with. A deeply intersectional understanding of trauma and harm is imperative. Being highly empathetic, well trained and seasoned both in the industry and in the field will support you in knowing when to change gears and when certain concepts don't apply.

Lastly, dear Intimacy Coordinator – be ferocious with the care of yourself through this work. Explore your own ritual and container work. If you carry your own personal experience of trauma, you must know when those triggers are neutralized, and there is absolutely nothing wrong with knowing you're not quite there yet. This field can be taxing and can be lonely – ask for peer support. We need you, and we must find a way for this work to be sustainable.

A Conversation with Olivia Luccardi

Brooke M. Haney

> Olivia Luccardi played Melissa on *The Deuce* on HBO, which in 2018, for its second season, was the first television show to hire an intimacy coordinator. This was a catalyst for the inclusion of intimacy coordinators in TV and film. In 2023, when Olivia played Officer Brandy Quinlan in *East New York* on CBS, she requested an intimacy coordinator for her first scene involving intimacy in the show. Mike Robin, one of the producers, is incredibly supportive of the intimacy movement, and set this as a precedent that was honored for all the other actors in the show.

BROOKE   Sometimes actors worry that if they articulate their boundaries, they might lose work. Have you ever felt that?

OLIVIA   I have always been nervous about that. I mean, there's always many things where it's like, "If I say this, will I lose my job? Or will they look down on me?" But at the same time, if they're not going to respect your boundaries and your body, then you don't need to work for those people.

BROOKE   I always think that you need to teach your body that it can trust you, that you will say no to things that don't work for you, then it can relax and be an instrument for your best work. So tell me, when the producers of *East New York* came to you, and asked if you wanted an intimacy coordinator for the first scene with your

	character in bed with Lavel Schley's character, even though you knew that it would be a kiss at most, why did you request an IC?
OLIVIA	I wanted to start a precedent, because I really do believe in the intimacy coordination movement. I think that they are really important to this industry, because for years, there were these awkward times that we just kind of bit our lip, shut up and did our job.
BROOKE	You were one of the first actors to work with an intimacy coordinator, when Alicia Rodis started working with *The Deuce* on HBO. What was that like for you, having already worked on lots of scenes of intimacy in both TV and film?
OLIVIA	Yeah, Alicia came on during season two. Before that, even though we didn't exactly have intimacy coordination, we did have some protocols, but Alicia just made it better and a lot more comfortable. When you have such a huge caliber of creators and actors that you're working with, you don't want to seem like you're intimidated or something, so it was really great.
BROOKE	When was the first time you worked with her on a big scene?
OLIVIA	Season three, the very first scene back.
BROOKE	What was it about her process that really worked for you?
OLIVIA	The scene was supposed to be like shooting a movie. I was moleskinned up, it was almost like there was Novocaine in my crotch. You could not feel anything. And we did have choreography for that scene. It was just knowing that we had an advocate there for us if we weren't comfortable.
BROOKE	Were there times before working with Alicia where you were uncomfortable?
OLIVIA	An example: in the first season I had this scene with this guy. He was a newer actor, great, kind guy. You know, it's one of his first jobs and it's a sex scene, day player as a sex scene. So that's awkward for everyone. And it took so long. We're fake fucking, fake fucking, fake fucking. We had to keep going for a long time – lines weren't right, this and that. Then at one point, "The bed is too bouncy. You have to kind of grind more, it looks too fake." There's a larger guy on top of me, and I'm hyperventilating over here.
BROOKE	Were you hyperventilating because it was so athletic and you were out of breath? Or because of what was going on emotionally?
OLIVIA	Athletic and out of breath. The guy easily had an extra 30 to 50 pounds on me. And then you know, sex is very breathy, fake or not. And it was just a long time, like four and a half hours. It would have been great, knowing that I could have spoken up and

	said, "I'm done." But you know, if we had Alicia there, it could have been looking at Alicia and she could have said it for me.
BROOKE	Besides TV, you've worked on intimacy in a number of indie films, right? What was that like?
OLIVIA	The sad fact is not everyone can have intimacy coordination because of budgets. And it's not like it's a mandatory thing yet, which it should be. They should make it work so that indie movies can afford an intimacy coordinator, because that's also where some of the weirdest shit happens and some of my weirdest experiences have happened.

I've had some really, bad, bad experiences; I've done a lot of indies. This isn't the indies' faults. I had one actor, we were about to have a sex scene, and he just asked, "You mind if I first show my Michaelangelo?" And I'm like, "I don't know what that is. Sure, whatever, do what you need." And he pulled his pants down. So I'm like, "Oh, my God, that means your dick. Your dick is out." But this was also before knowing about intimacy coordination. Now I would have spoken up and been like, "Nope, put some pants on. Put some pants on, old man." But I didn't know that at the time. |
BROOKE	That's such a huge part of an IC's job, in the beginning, to clarify for everyone what's expected and what the boundaries are, so that something like that doesn't happen.
OLIVIA	I mean, he's a veteran actor, but this was his first love scene ever. So he didn't have the knowledge either.
BROOKE	Yes, assuming that because someone has been in the business a long time they automatically know what to expect from a scene of intimacy is wrong and can lead to serious miscommunication.
OLIVIA	I had another experience, not that long ago, where because of my knowledge, from reading about it and keeping up with you guys and the work that you're doing, I was able to speak up and be like, "I am not feeling it. I'm done." Literally, during the filming, it was hours of this intimate scene that they looked at me and asked, "How are you doing?" I was like, "I have one more in me."

And he was like, "Okay", we did one more. And that was it. And from that I learned to speak up before I hit my wall, because I spoke up once I hit my wall. |
| BROOKE | How can you tell you're about to hit your wall? |
| OLIVIA | I don't know, still learning that. I think it's something that just the industry has to start moving toward, that intimacy coordinators |

are required on every set. That, you know, just like actors are paid for, like super low budget, somebody might make, like $100 a day. There should be intimacy coordinators that are on those sort of SAG budgets just to make it possible for everyone to have it.

BROOKE A lot of us will work for a lower wage on an indie project. There could be an argument you shouldn't produce a film that you can't afford to do safely, and I think there can be a range that makes it affordable.

OLIVIA Yeah, yeah. You're right. We shouldn't, but at the same time, the industry should change its standards and make it affordable.

BROOKE Absolutely. What would be your advice to an early career actor about how to handle a scene of intimacy?

OLIVIA Don't be afraid to speak up for your boundaries, and how you're feeling. That's really for me the biggest thing, speak up, make sure you're comfortable. If you're not, say you're not and find ways that you guys can all work to fix it and make it comfortable. But then also, it's all awkward. Just make it like a dance. You know, it is choreographed.

BROOKE Let's all admit it's awkward. If we start from that, "Look, this is weird, but let's choreograph it, let's make it that dance," then we can move through the awkwardness and we can all do our job.

OLIVIA Exactly.

BROOKE Different actors like different levels of choreography. Some actors prefer every moment choreographed down to specific counts. And some people want to know, "You're gonna go from this position to this position to this position," and then they want to find their way. How do you like to work?

OLIVIA I personally like trying to figure it out with the partner, that there's an open line of communication. I've been in indie movies for so long and we don't have an intimacy coordinator, so I find my path. I like to just make sure that it's comfortable.

BROOKE Do you have an example?

OLIVIA Like with kissing it's always sort of like, "I am going to kiss you. Are you okay with that? Don't worry, I'm not gonna stick my tongue in your mouth, but like, I'm gonna actually kiss you. Are you okay with that? If you're not, I won't." I like to have an open line of communication and sort of figure it out with my partner. I like having an intimacy coordinator there if there's a point that I don't feel comfortable enough to speak out, or if I don't like the way this scene is going.

Intimacy and Dance 16

Brooke M. Haney with contributions from Sarah Lozoff and Nicole Perry

> In 2020, Oregon Shakespeare Festival made Sarah Lozoff their resident intimacy director, the first in America for a major theatre company. Additionally, she was named one of 2021 Broadway Women's Fund's *Women to Watch on Broadway*. However, one of the primary ways that she has innovated the intimacy industry has been with her work in dance as both the first intimacy director at American Ballet Theatre (ABT) and resident intimacy director for RudduR Dance. Sarah shared her thoughts with me on intimacy and dance and I will pass them onto you in this chapter. Sarah's work with RudduR Dance has included mostly new work and, by contrast, ABT has a deep repertoire of old ballets, so Sarah has had the opportunity to work with dancers on their boundaries in a variety of contexts.

Main Themes That Arise In This Work

Dancers as a group of performing artists can experience significant dichotomy. Dancers typically have incredible agency and mastery over their own bodies. They're incredibly aware of and understand what their bodies can take and how far they can push them physically in order to maximize their growth zone, and yet often it is dancers who seem to feel or experience the least amount of agency and autonomy over their own bodies as far as what is done to them, put on them and around the power dynamics in the industry. Dancers are by and large a group of performing artists whose voices have been literally trained out of them from very young ages, as, while training, they are not allowed to speak for hours at a time.

Cultural Context

Due to its roots, the dance world is incredibly hierarchical. Sarah primarily works in concert dance: ballet and concert ballet, which originated in the courts. In 1581, ballet made what is considered to be its debut with *La Ballet Comique de la Reine.* This is credited to Catherine de Medici, wife of King Henri II of France, who introduced Italy's *ballet de cour* (court dancing) to the French court. In the seventeenth century, ballet performances were still only for the aristocracy. Professional performers were only allowed to dance roles of the peasant or servant, never a hero, king or person of high birth. Those roles were danced by the aristocracy until King Louis XIV created a professional training academy, the Académie Royale de Danse. As a result, we still have a significant class or tiered system within most ballet companies. While folks tend to be friendly and may co-mingle socially, these power dynamics can make a huge difference in who feels they can contribute in rehearsal, and what they feel they can consent and dissent to.

Navigating Boundaries

When selecting a strategy for navigating boundaries in dance, consider time. Some contracts will stipulate that dancers can't be asked to work, even to have meetings with the intimacy director, before they are on contract. Once dancers are on contract, their rehearsal schedule can be incredibly demanding. In rehearsal, especially for a historical ballet with established choreography, it may not be necessary nor an effective use of time to ask a dancer if they are okay with every move, every lift. However, they still get to set their boundaries.

> In concert dance, choreographers often require performers to crack open their lives to extreme depths to be the conceptual fodder for the choreography itself. This can mean that dancers end up revisiting distressing psychosomatic states in rehearsal and performance. The choreographer–dancer power dynamic can reinforce these expectations so that dancers feel unable to create or assert boundaries surrounding sharing their life experiences. Developing boundary setting processes and check-ins for how much, and to what depths, dancers share of themselves through rehearsal AND performance is imperative for ethical work.
>
> Britta Joy Peterson, intimacy coordinator/director and choreographer, New York City

If a dancer has a physical boundary, it's important to ask if this is a boundary for today or if it is ongoing, as that will let the choreographer know if they need to change the choreography or simply adjust for the rehearsal.

Dancers are typically excellent at recognizing what is going on in their bodies physically, what their limitations are and how far they can push their bodies. It can be much harder to recognize and voice boundaries around mental and emotional wellness. However, if the ID can connect mental and emotional health to the already keen awareness of the physical body, it can help in realizing that the skillset they already possess can be simply expanded upon to include other important aspects of health and wellness.

The Rehearsal Process

Whether the intimacy director gets 10 min to introduce themselves or 60–90 minutes for a workshop, letting the dancers know you are available for the duration of the contract and how to get a hold of you is key. Sometimes this works even better for dancers than pre-production meetings, because there can be a learning curve and they have a better sense of what they can ask about or talk to the ID about once the process gets underway.

It can be challenging to figure out how much time to spend on the story and on what may be coming up for the dancers emotionally. Sometimes dancers will need tools to bring themselves and their experiences to the work, and sometimes they will need tools to leave their work on the floor when rehearsal is over. They aren't used to sitting around and talking. Sometimes they just need to dance. Often dancers will use dancing to work through something, and it can be a coping mechanism to simply push it all down. So some flexibility may be needed to figure out how much time to set aside for all of this.

Sarah strongly recommends a daily tap in/tap out. Things come up and it can be a whirlwind of emotions, so we don't want to be causal. It's important to mark when the work begins and ends. It's also good for community building. When possible, she likes to have a check in at the top of rehearsal and saves up to 10 minutes at the end for closure.

Barriers

It is good practice to offer barriers. They are incredibly easy to sew into leotards or dance belts, and wardrobe and costumes are usually very collaborative in these cases. Many dancers are desensitized in those areas and feel that their costume is enough. It's important, however, to have these conversations privately and be prepared to consider requiring barriers if someone in the ensemble requests it.

Be Aware

If you are coming into dance from another intimacy specialty, it is important to note some differences in order to not inadvertently step on toes. For example, especially in theatre, the ID is often a part of the movement team, and may choreograph significant moments in the show. However, in dance it is all movement, it's all choreography. Coming in as a movement specialist can create defensiveness, because in dance the choreographer, whose vision is being realized much like the role of the director in theatre, is a movement specialist. It's useful as a movement specialist, or especially as a dancer, to have a shared vocabulary. However, in a dance space, the scope of practice of the ID can sometimes be limited to boundaries, consent, closure practices and small ways to make physical intimacy pop.

> ### A Note on Academic Dance
>
> Since dance training, making and performing are not free of power, we must seek to strategically disrupt the power dynamics in our rooms. An emphasis on performer agency to give consent

to touch-based teaching practices and/or to choreographic choices would disrupt the traditionally hierarchical and patriarchal structures of dance companies in which the artistic director, followed by the choreographer, is the voice of power. The same is true of academic dance departments and even studios, where the title of professor, guest artist or simply teacher creates power dynamics.

Nicole Perry

From Nicole: Students start taking dance as young as two. A child this young is just gaining bodily control and might not even know when to go to the bathroom. Dance teachers are given the power over even these decisions. Teachers controlling both bodies and the space is built into the pedagogy. Meanwhile, historically, the teaching of dance accepts touch in an unspoken way, so conversations about boundaries just aren't had.

This kind of bodily control is mirrored in school, academically. Middle school children's bodies are especially monitored and controlled. By the time students get to college, they have been indoctrinated from age two in dance and age six in school, so they don't believe us when we say they can have boundaries. We will be undoing years of indoctrination, so they likely won't feel comfortable saying "no" right away. It might start with something as simple as learning they can get up and go to the bathroom without asking. They will watch to see validation when a "no" is offered to see if they can trust that they truly have agency in the space.

Nicole recommends having a "touch policy." Currently, she teaches without touch. However, students can ask for touch if that is how they learn best. If she does choose to touch a student in order to demonstrate something, she is clear about the learning goal. She explicitly explains which parts of her body will touch which parts of the student's body and for what purpose. Then, she asks for a volunteer. She always gives options. For example, if she is teaching weight sharing, and a student had a boundary around touch that day, they can choose to use an exercise ball.

If you are a teacher who still uses touch in your pedagogy, she offers the use of "consent cards." She went to a craft store, bought cute door hangers, and wrote yes on one side and no on the other. They can be hung on a bar in a ballet class or laid on the floor in front of a dancer in a modern class to indicate if the dancer wishes to be touched that day or given adjustments with words instead. In the past, she's used these consent cards to take attendance and it has allowed her to see which students always say "yes" or always say "no." This gives her insight into potential conversations to bring up around risk taking. For example, if a student has never said "no," how will they know they are able to? It might feel risky to them to try and school is an excellent place to try something that feels scary.

Bibliography

Minden, Eliza. (2014) "Courtly Origins." *dancer.com*, https://dancer.com/ballet-info/the-story-of-ballet/courtly-origins-de-medici-and-king-louis-xiv/?v=7516fd43adaa.

Perry, Nicole. (2021) "Power Dynamics in Dance." *Danceguist Magazine*, February.

A Conversation with Jimmy Smits

Brooke M. Haney

> Jimmy Smits is a Golden Globe, Emmy and SAG Award winning actor, whose career has spanned decades. Perhaps best known for his role on *NYPD Blue*, he has significant experience working in the industry on scenes of intimacy. Imagine my delight when I found out I got to be Jimmy's first intimacy coordinator. Jimmy expressed enthusiasm right off the bat about using the IC not only for boundaries, but to make the intimacy as real as possible. We worked together on *East New York* where he played Officer Suarez. Kelly Hu joined him for these scenes as Allison Cha. We did two episodes that included intimacy in season one. The first was directed by Sharon Lewis and the second by Mo McRae. Jimmy graciously agreed to talk with me about his experience working with an IC and how the industry has changed since the introduction of intimacy coordinators.

BROOKE   Your experience is really interesting, because you've had such a long career, and you've worked on lots of scenes involving intimacy. And now, here you are working with an intimacy coordinator for the first time.

JIMMY   I think it's invaluable, what we can learn and how we can make the art better with it.

BROOKE That's the key, how can we make the art better? Tell me a little bit about how the industry was different for you back with *NYPD Blue* and other shows before the #metoo movement and intimacy coordinators.

JIMMY So I don't want to say it was a free for all, but it depended. On *Blue* there was an opportunity, not only with language, but with intimacy to kind of push the envelope a little bit with what we were able to do. That was the first time that was happening for network television, and there were all kinds of parameters that the producers had with the network. That, in and of itself, created some built in guardrails of what you were able to show. And you know, you always start out with this, "We're going to be protected," right?

Whether it's a fight choreography scene or you're working with children, or you're working with animals, whatever, you have these people that are supposed to be watching over the safety issues. When you don't have that with regards to intimacy, sometimes, even with the best intention, you literally feel exposed.

BROOKE I think you're really keying into something. TV is a very fast-paced environment and time can make really good intentions become coercive, because we're fighting light, or we're going into overtime or whatever.

JIMMY I'll go back to *Blue*, because there were certain parameters and we choreographed a lot of stuff. Because of the fact that you weren't able to show things, it necessitated a collaboration and talk about how we were going to maneuver it. But, I mean, you're trusting that the director was looking out for all these things. And then I think as we went on, it got less specific, and you just kind of assume, because of television being a flowing process, that everybody was okay with it. And that might not have been the case. So I think just by experiencing our relationship, what happened with us, it's an invaluable thing to have another person to bounce off of there.

BROOKE The director has a lot on their plate. They are watching for everything. And another way an IC can support the project is by being on monitor. We watch to make sure that nothing is showing that hasn't been agreed to and we're watching the story through the lens of touch. We ask ourselves, are we telling this story in a compelling way? What's the most helpful thing for you that an IC can do to help you as an actor?

JIMMY   The whole dynamic of being able to talk about boundaries, and how we get to a certain place to achieve a certain visual kind of look, was very helpful for me. And then with the guys, there's an assumption that, you know, it's okay for us because we're guys. It's like, no, no, no.

BROOKE Everyone deserves to have their boundaries heard and honored. It's really problematic when the assumption is that the IC is there to make women feel safe.

JIMMY   Yeah. Rightfully so, because of the transgressions throughout our industry's history. And again, going back to specifically on *Blue*, it was a bit of a boys club. We had to kind of be like, "Guys it's a closed set. No, people can't come down from the office to check in to see the tone of the scene." It's all those little kinds of things that you had to stay on top of, which the intimacy coordinator would take that onus off. And I think it helps the artistic collaborative process immensely.

BROOKE As far as the storytelling, how does having an intimacy choreographer or coordinator impact your processes as an actor?

JIMMY   I guess it has to do with the collaboration effect. It's the brushstroke that I refer to that just keeps washing over me, that you really feel like there's somebody that's specifically looking out for this area. And because, you know, we're doing an approximation of what human life is supposed to be, right? So when we get to this issue of intimacy as well, it's the same kind of thing in a different way, heightened.

BROOKE Speaking of telling stories about human life, one of the things that was important to us when we were working on our scene with Kelly Hu on *East New York* was showing the difference in generation around intimacy. Why is it important for intimacy to look different over different generations? And why is it important to have representation of more than just a very young generation?

JIMMY   I love the fact that now the intimacy coordinator can participate with that aspect of it. Intergenerational, you know, as we as a society progresses into this area of being more inclusive, I'm talking with age, with race, with your sexual identity, fluidity, all those kinds of things. We're able to get to a more realistic approach, I think, of what we're supposed to be representing. Our industry has a kind of history of defining. Media, in general, has a powerful effect on society. And this art form, whether it be film or television, impacts society in a lot of different ways. You specifically

	asked about intergenerational, you know, meaning older people, and being able to show that in a realistic kind of way, but I think it applies totally across the board.
BROOKE	Media is instructive and if we only show the same thing over and over again, it seems like that's the only thing that exists.
JIMMY	Or from a particular point of view, right?
BROOKE	Exactly. Okay, when we were choreographing, did you prefer how we worked with Sharon, where we'd choreographed it very specifically: beats, counts, where hands went, everything? Or did you enjoy how we worked with Mo, where we're very sure to establish the boundaries between you and Kelly, and create a kind of outline to the scene, but then the two of you really found it organically as actors. What worked best for your process?
JIMMY	I'm not going to hedge on this, because I don't think that we should get into, like, a hard and fast rule about it.
BROOKE	Agreed.
JIMMY	Choreography really helps, because it is a kind of dance with the camera. So there are little telltale things that you do. I mean, the simple thing of having a kiss with somebody, and knowing how to pivot and tilt so that the camera can capture stuff is hugely helpful. And again, especially when you asked specifically about the two different scenarios that we shot together, one was a pretty standard simple kiss. But it came at the beginning of these two characters' relationship. And then it was these two actors who were involved in the scene, you know, they had just started working with each other as well. (I'm talking third person.) So I think that the choreography was very valuable, because the choreography helped to tell the story of subtext.

And with regards to the other scene that we shot afterwards, there was an aspect of it at some point in time that was not as choreographed, but we talked about boundaries, and how we would, where we would want to go and what we were comfortable doing. So there was a kind of not choreography, but there were parameters that were kind of set so that there was a comfort level. To establish the comfort levels in all this, again, is invaluable. |
| BROOKE | There are people in the industry, who have been working a long time, as you have, who haven't worked with an IC yet. For some people, there can be a fear that the IC is coming in to be the sex police, or they're afraid that we will take a piece of the project |

that is theirs. What's advice that you would give to an actor who's been in business a long time and is getting to work with an IC for the first time?

JIMMY You have to kind of open yourself up to what is a primary North Star, as far as I'm concerned, in the business, which is the collaborative process. That has to be your jump point. There's a lot of people in this business that feel like, "Art is *my* thing. I'm giving you my art and you try to capture it the way you can." But no, the bottom line is, it is a collaborative process, especially in film and television, when you have electronic things, apparatus, that are trying to capture that kind of reality.

Keeping that open, that artistic openness in terms of the lines of communication, is of paramount importance. And so I think that the coordinator also needs to have the language to be able to facilitate it to make the director feel like they're still part – it's just another lane. It might feel a little bit open, but we're all shooting for that specific point that we want to get to. Let's do everything we can to make the art as beautiful as possible and as real as possible.

Prosthetics   17

Amanda Liz Cutting

> Amanda Liz Cutting is a certified intimacy coordinator and intimacy director with Intimacy Directors International (IDI), works on various National Society of Intimacy Professionals (NSIP) committees and leads Principal Intimacy Professionals (PIP). In 2019, she was the first intimacy coordinator to be hired by Bollywood for the web series Mastram (MX Player), which has become the highest-viewed series in the world with 616 million views. I first met Amanda when I took a class from her on prosthetics. Her clarity as a teacher impressed me. While she has many other areas of expertise, I felt this book would really benefit from her knowledge on prosthetics, so I was thrilled when she agreed to write.

Content Note: In this chapter, we will use anatomical terms for the body and genitalia regarding prosthetics and pubic wigs.

Definitions

Prosthetic makeup

Also called **special makeup effects** and **FX prosthesis**, uses sculpting, moulding and casting techniques to create advanced cosmetic effects. These pieces

DOI: 10.4324/9781003410553-31

are placed in addition to a person's body to act as an extension of their character (https://dbpedia.org/page/Prosthetic_makeup).

Lifecasting

The process of taking a mould of the actor's face, head or body part to create a duplicate of the part or provide a template for unique pieces to be built.

Alginate

A soft, flexible silicone rubber used in casting.

"World of the Show"

The universe in which the story takes place. It may borrow from history, cultures and styles. The world is all details, from the colour pallet to how the characters relate and interact. The show will impact many creative departments, including how intimacy and intimate actions are defined.

MUFX

Makeup Special Effects is a department in the cinematic industry that works with specialized prosthetics and makeup effects to create a desired image.

Foundational Knowledge

What Is a Prosthetic in Film/TV/Theatre Context?

A prosthetic may augment, distort or replace an element of the body. They can be used in medical scenes depicting surgeries, deliveries of babies, intimacy scenes to replace or cover a performer's genitalia, and in fantasy to create different appendages or orifices.

How is a Prosthetic Created?

Often beginning with concept art derived from research and consultation with "the world of the show" and the director's vision, a production artist or designer will create these designs and bring them to production for approval.

These drawings are often done before casting, and additional consideration may be needed to adapt the design to accommodate the performer's needs and boundaries before a potential life casting occurs.

Are Prosthetics Always Custom-made?

No. Often SFX companies will have a storage full of different bodies, parts of bodies like the torso, limbs, organs, eyes, wounds and gore effects, and even babies and young children at various stages of development. These can be utilized for multiple shows, painted or recast, to represent different skin tones and textures (in the case of SIFI). They can also be custom-made for the specific needs of a scene or in cases where identical representation is needed cast from the performer's body directly.

What Are the Considerations to Have in Mind When Working With Adhesives and Prosthetics?

- Adhesive allergies.
- Latex allergies.
- Sensitive or thin skin areas.
- Current abrasions/injuries with wounds healing.
- Gluten allergies.
- Vegan options to support performers' personal choice.
- No skin peels, skin spa treatments in the last two days.
- Application of the prosthetic can take as much time to remove as it did to get into in.

Intimacy Professionals' Considerations and Prep

The following are notes and points for conversation with the different parties involved with prosthetics.

Production

- Conversation with the director for the vision of the scene
  - Shot lists, storyboards, previs videos
- Do riders need to be created?
- If depicting breasts, buttocks or genitalia, YES. *Note: the performer should approve the representation of their body part even if the prosthetic is used on a body double or stunt performer in the scene.*

MUFX

- Have a conversation with the MUFX department to understand their process and the needs of MUFX of the performer. Note: *MUFX will contact the performer and review much of this or the AD team. However, it is information you should have about any intimate body part casting.*
- Seeing a copy of the design may also support understanding.
- Clarify if shaving is needed (often it is not required, shortly trimmed body hair is sufficient).
- Clarify the duration of the casting.
- Clarify what items a performer needs to bring and what will be provided.
- Clarify if a merkin will also be used.

Performer

- Be clear as to what is being cast.
- They can ask for an advocate in space.
- Let them know makeup FX will be calling to go over the details.
- Give an overview of the process.
- Inform how much time it will take to cast.
- Clarify that medical garments and protective gear will be provided.
- Inform them to make sure to wear appropriate clothing.
- Answer questions about needing to shave/hair.
   - Vaseline or a release will be placed in advance.
- Inform how MUFX will maintain a little physical touch, so they know who's around them.
- You may need to ask specific, more delicate questions such as:
   - Is what is being created an accurate representation of their body?
   - Clarifying things like circumcision for persons with a penis.
   - Pubic hair amount and grooming.

Types of Intimate Prosthetics

Below are two types of prosthetics an IP may be involved in coordinating and specific considerations when working with them.

Merkins (Pubic Wigs)

The history of the merkin dates as far as the 1450s and was used to hide the lack of hair on the genitals due to the area being shaved to prevent the spread of lice or because of disease. All sexes would utilize these pubic wigs. The wealthy wear these, sometimes groomed in a particular fashion, to display privilege and "health" enough to maintain it. During Shakespeare's time, a generous and amply fluffed merkin was used to disguise a man's penis when required to perform nude and portray a female character. In our current cinematic culture, merkins may be used for numerous reasons, to be historically accurate, to disguise a performer's existing pubic hair and to facilitate ease of applying a prosthetic.

Specific Intimacy Professionals' Considerations

- If this is a period piece where the genitals are shown, you may need to clarify if the type of pubic hair and amount is relevant to "the world" with production.
- Possibly check whether the performer consents to their pubic hair being filmed or prefers a merkin.
  - Also, what form of grooming they have done, as it is relevant to "the world."
  - Research as to the current fashion of pubic hair of the time may be needed.
  - Performer approval on representation.
- Some personal grooming may be needed for ease of application and removal.
- Reminder to not exfoliate in the application area a week before.
- Reminder about abstaining from alcohol the night before as that can affect the natural oils in the skin and reduce the glue's effectiveness.

Process of Application

- Skin will be cleaned and primed for application.
- A fabric modesty barrier or an entire tape piece or modesty plate will be used as the first barrier before applying the wig.
- We may need to incorporate a barrier into the garment should there be intimate action.
- After the modesty application, makeup will blend with the modesty garment.

- Then the merkin (wig) will be applied.
- Additional makeup touch-up and grooming of the wig.

Prosthetic Penises

Historically, the penis has been replicated for centuries; be it stone, plaster, wood or rare gems, civilization has created them. The earliest strap-on prosthetic was recorded from the Upper Paleolithic period, c.10,000 BC. Penis substitutes have been used throughout history for many reasons, including same-sex intimacies and a device to support those with erectile dysfunction.

Now, in the cinematic world, if the penis has a function in the scene, it must be a prosthetic for the performers' safety and ease of continuity. For further clarity, an organic penis that is erect can not be shown on screen as it is deemed a "sex act." Additionally, actors will not have their actual member cast. The pelvic area may be moulded to support a firm fitting of the inorganic penis; however, these prosthetic penises are, in essence, an artistic representation.

Intimacy Professionals' Considerations

- If this is a period piece where the genitals will be shown, you may need to clarify if the type of pubic hair and amount is relevant to "the world" with production.
    - This may mean the addition of a merkin.
- Reminder to not exfoliate in the application area a week before.
- Some personal landscaping for the performer may be needed for glue adherence.
- Reminder to not drink alcohol the night before due to adhesives.
- Performer approval of representation.
- A sensitive conversation about whether they would prefer representation circumcised or not. *Note: Refer to Chapter 11, "Queer Intimacy," for additional notes regarding packers, strap-ons and dildos for extra sensitivity and considerations.*

Process of Application

- A performer will be fitted in a modesty garment with a slight tucking aspect.

- Then the prosthetic will be placed over the top of the garment.
- The wig may be already punched into the prosthetic or additionally applied.
- Makeup and hair will be a part of blending skin tone etc.

Choreography with a prosthetic

When working with strap-ons, dildos or other sex toys, ensure the object is asked for in a desexualized manner. An offer is to call it "the devise" or "device and harness" to allow the desexualization of the object. When using a strap-on, remove it from the harness to provide cast and crew comfort between takes where possible.

Treat a prosthetic like any other organic body part regarding choreography. Masking is always an option; however, if actual physical actions occur to the prosthetic, such as oral or hand stroking, additional considerations may be needed for lubrication as the prosthetic has no oils or moisture. Checking in with MUFX as to what lubricants would be best before offering. Awareness that oral stimulation on a prosthetic may be considered "real sex" to some. Limit the takes of real-time action occurring and utilize masking and camera angles where possible.

The device has no physical feedback to the performer wearing it, so choreography may require an anchor point elsewhere on the actor's body to help with rhythm and storytelling moment. For example, a forearm on an upper thigh or a hand grasping a hip. The importance of eye contact for key signalling moments while layering in breath and body tension in both persons in action will be essential in creating a believable scene. For moments of climax and orgasm, tensing the glutes and abdominals while shifting some weight to the balls of the feet may support the representation of this occurring.

Rehearsals

Utilizing a prosthetic may require more time for blocking. Look to set up a rehearsal outside of shooting if intimate action occurs to the prosthetic to choreograph the moments adequately. If working with an inorganic penis, attempt to have one at rehearsal to work with. It is essential to frontload this need to the relevant departments in advance for planning and the performers to set up expectations.

Introduction to Part Three
Looking Forward
Brooke M. Haney

Thank you for taking the time to read this book. Now that you've explored specialties, let's take a look forward to the future of the industry.

In Part Three, Ann James and I will talk about the training and purpose of intimacy captains. We started the book talking about the area where an intimacy professional should be competent, and here we will discuss how to determine qualification. The ideas in this chapter can be applied to your work overall or in a specialty. We all set up our best practices, and, in the moment, we must learn to adapt them to the folks and situation in the rehearsal room or on set. The last thing we want is to be so rigid that we don't listen. Laura Rikard will guide you through ideas for adapting your process to individual actors. Finally, I invited any of the writers who had time for a conversation about our thoughts on where the intimacy industry is at and our hopes for the future.

I hope you enjoy these last tidbits of knowledge. There is so much to still discover in this industry. I hope to be in a room or on set someday learning from you.

Things to Consider

For Intimacy Professionals

- How do you evaluate which projects you are qualified for?

- What examples do you have of times you've adapted your process?
- What do you hope the industry looks like in 10 years?

For Directors and Producers

- How do you break down a project around its intimacy needs??
- What questions will you ask an intimacy professional in an interview to make sure they are the right fit for a particular project?
- How do you describe your process around intimate scenes in order to make sure you get to work with an intimacy professional that is best for your process?

For Actors

- What intimacy professional skills most compliment your process?
- Is being an intimacy captain something that interests you and do you feel well suited to support an intimacy choreographer?
- Do you feel comfortable advocating for yourself to your intimacy professional so that you get the most out of that working relationship?
- How do you feel about where the industry is at around this role, and what do you hope the future looks like?

Intimacy Captain

18

Brooke M. Haney with contributions from Ann James

> The role of intimacy captain is a competency that an actor can have to be an additional asset to a production. The idea of an intimacy captain was a pretty natural leap; theatre already utilizes fight captains and dance captains. Ann James, founder of Intimacy Coordinators of Color, was in talks with two AEA delegates about defining intimacy practice as a whole for the industry when they started thinking about the need for trained intimacy captains.
>
> In April 2021, Intimacy Coordinators of Color (ICOC) began offering an intimacy captain certificate and, at the time of our interview, they had trained over 700 intimacy captains. I sat down with Ann to learn more about what they saw as the role of the intimacy captain (ICap) in a theatre production and what training entails.

Recognizing the load put on a stage management team, and the fact that the intimacy professional would likely come and go throughout the production process, a support position was needed. "At ICOC we believe that this emerging position will help develop new language around consent in the rehearsal space," Ann explained. "We celebrate that ICaps also provide more freedom for highly utilized stage management teams."

Ideally, a production should start to think about their intimacy captain as early as when they are auditioning. Ann encourages actors to put intimacy

DOI: 10.4324/9781003410553-33

captain on their resume to let directors know that they have this expertise and experience. Directors and producers can also consult with the intimacy professional (IP) for the show, once it has been cast, to see if they have insight into who would be a good fit for the role.

The Intimacy Captain in Rehearsal

- Checks in with the actors.
- May lead and supervise the boundary check in.
- Learns the IP's language and communicates using that vocabulary.
- Takes copious notes.
- May lead the cool down at the end of the day.

At Tech

- At this point, the boundary check in should be built into the warm up.
- As an actor in the show, the intimacy captain should focus on their own needs and responsibilities.
- If more is needed, the professional IC should leave the captain with very clear instructions.

During the Run

- Runs the intimacy call.
  - Much like a fight call, an intimacy call is there to get the choreography back into the actor's bodies and should be done incrementally. First, it will be run at quarter speed, simply to review it. Then at half speed, with attention to levels of pressure and breath. Finally, run it at three quarters speed with full acting.
- Keeps an ear out for if anyone is feeling ill.
  - If someone is, they consult with the stage manager about whether or not the cast needs to go to design B for any scenes. Design B is an alternate choreography that the intimacy professional has put into place in the event that the full choreography can't be performed and the production needs to tell the story in a different way.
- Has an awareness of what is happening backstage.
  - Is everyone checking in? It can be natural for actors to start to assume that their partner's boundaries will always be the same and therefore they don't need a check in every day. However, the ICap can remind

them that boundaries can be different day to day and that a consent-forward production makes the space for that to be expressed.
- Are boundaries being honored on stage and off?
  - Communicates with the SM about things that can be put in the performance report for the intimacy professional.

Training Includes

- The ethos of being a good ICap.
- Defining boundaries, personal and professional.
- Theatrical Intimacy Education's vocabulary regarding fences and gates.
- How to show up in the room.
- An approach that centers on identifying people properly.
- Learning how to communicate with the stage management team.
- How to take intimacy choreography notes.
- What to include in the ICap log.

So What Makes a Good Intimacy Captain?

A good ICap is a good listener, an excellent observer, a leader who watches before contributing. They should be actively working as an actor so that they are already familiar with production and are ready to take on an additional role. Familiarity with the language and vocabulary that intimacy coordinators use is essential. It's a position of service; different IPs need different things from an intimacy captain, so the captain needs to be able to observe the IP's style and flow with it. They should be detail oriented and an excellent note taker who is able to adapt their note-taking style to that of the intimacy choreographer. At the end of each rehearsal, they fill out an ICap log.

An actor that is interested in becoming an intimacy professional in the future might choose to become an intimacy captain first to begin to think about production through that lens while still pursuing their acting career. It is an excellent way to support a culture of consent.

Qualification 19

Brooke M. Haney

> A note to be clear about my personal bias: at the time of writing this chapter, I am intentionally not certified. I am also not connected to any training program, though I have taken classes with many of them because I believe in the necessity of ongoing learning and value a diversity of thought in our field. I was one of the first 50 people who joined the SAG-AFTRA registry, a list of "qualified intimacy professionals." I did this knowing that, right or wrong, it provided a shorthand with which I could assure potential employers of my training and experience.

The SAG-AFTRA Registry and Certification

While not certification, the SAG-AFTRA intimacy coordinator registry is a list that "builds on the Standards and Protocols for the Use of Intimacy Coordinators originally introduced in January 2020." The requirements to get on this list and how those were selected and evaluated has not always been transparent. Additionally, being on this list simply indicates that an intimacy coordinator has trained in certain areas and worked on SAG-AFTRA projects for at least 60 or 75 days, depending on the year they applied. There is currently nothing similar for theater.

There are many excellent training organizations around the world that teach skills in intimacy direction and coordination. Several of them offer certification to folks who have completed a certain level of training. There are many considerations around the value and ethics of certification, and I'm not going to go into them here. If you're interested in that, see Chelsea Pace's thoughtful article "The Certification Question" in the *Journal for Consent-Based Performance*, as well as Jessica Steinrock's blog entry "The Certification Question: A Response" on the Intimacy Directors and Coordinators website, to decide what aligns with your personal values and training needs as well as what will set you up for the best chance of success in this industry.

International Considerations

From Cessalee Stovall: In many ways an intimacy professionals' skills and credentials may be received differently in a country that has a different emphasis on learning and community or collective knowledge. The certification question is a nuanced conversation when working in an international context. The global uptake on intimacy direction and intimacy work has been as varied as the practice. The US and UK, as originators of the job title, were also the first countries to develop programs for training professionals. However, access to these training programs – particularly via the SAG-AFTRA certification approved organizations – is often extremely expensive due to fluctuations in exchange rates, is also inconvenient based on time zones and, with the barrier to global travel (and international flight-price hikes) due to Covid-19, they often omit the "hands on" / in the room process. These barriers can create a chasm in countries without their own certification process. Equating certification and qualification, particularly when you are outside of the certifier's domain, can insinuate that validation of expertise means more when it's obtained abroad. Considering the number of countries globally that are elder and community centric, the notion of knowledge requiring validation in the form of external approval can be problematic at best and violent at worst.

Qualification

As a new intimacy professional, it really is up to you to decide when you are qualified for your first job. I've been actively mentoring since 2018 and I have always left that decision up to my mentees. For some folks, that means starting on projects with low stakes, perhaps just a few kisses. You get to decide the best way for you to learn, when and how to transition into the workforce, and what projects you are ready to support. Robbie Taylor Hunt advises:

> [D]etermining whether you can handle a job might include reflecting on whether you've done something similar before, or reflecting on what you need to bridge the gap in your experience. Think about what feels like a safe level, stretch level, and dangerous/unsafe level in terms of your own capacity at any given time. It's never worth it pushing yourself to take a job, even if it feels really exciting, if you sense you're actually not ready or equipped at that time.

Considerations

Remember, you do not have to be ready for everything to be ready for something. That also means that being ready for some things doesn't mean you're ready for anything. Here are some things to consider.

Budget and Time: While a student or low budget independent film might seem like the ideal place to start out (and it might be), often these types of projects are trying to cut as many costs as possible and are really tight on time. These two things can make an IC's job exponentially more difficult. What might look like extreme efficiency to an experienced IC may feel rushed to a newer IC and not provide the time needed to process information and make informed decisions.

Location: An outdoor project, with weather variables and more possibility of interaction with the public, creates additional things to consider in your risk assessment than something in a studio, theater or on-location indoors.

Scale (financial): The nice thing about a student or low budget project is that the team is often quite small, providing more access to the director and fewer people with whom to coordinate. The other extreme, like Broadway, a network show or large budget film, increases the number of people you'll need to support. Additionally, larger projects are often higher profile, involving folks with even more power. If advocating to folks in power is a skill you are still honing, working at that level might not be best for your development.

Scale (artistic): Consider how many scenes of intimacy there are, how many actors in each scene and how many actors total. Will you be working with just principal actors, or are there background actors involved as well? Choreographing an orgy is very different from staging simulated sex between two people. Additionally, a scene with 30 nude background actors presents a challenge that a private scene of intimacy doesn't.

Content: Look at the level and amount of physical intimacy. Is there nudity and how familiar are you with riders? Do any scenes require a specialty? Is it something in which you have competence? If not, you may choose to bring in a consultant or pass the job to someone else. This might also be a great time to look for a mentor. Find someone who you know has the skills and ask them if they would be willing to work with you on the project or that particular scene so that you can learn from them.

On Mentorship

Several training programs offer mentorship. Outside of that, it can feel difficult to find a mentor. I and other intimacy professionals I know receive numerous requests for mentorship. Folks ask to shadow, assist, meet for coffee, etc. These requests also go up on discussion boards like Facebook intimacy groups regularly.

Mentorship can take a variety of forms from shadowing to assisting. I personally don't have folks only shadow me, because I believe everyone has something they can offer to the production and that learning by doing is incredibly valuable. Studying under a mentor or as an apprentice is a wonderful opportunity to get experience while honing your craft. If this is a goal of yours, here is some advice.

Research the person you want to work with. I've received emails from folks who have found my email address on the SAG-AFTRA registry. Many of these emails have a very generic request to be mentored and include generic questions like asking me if I live in their area. A very basic internet search reveals where I work, so that inquiry lets me know right away that they don't know anything about me, which means I have no idea if I am a good mentor for them. Find someone that is doing something that you admire, perhaps they are working in a specialty you are interested in pursuing. Maybe they have a similar identity to you and you would value learning from them how they navigate the industry.

When you reach out, be specific. Share where you are at in your training. Let them know why you are interested in working with them specifically and what you would like that mentorship to look like. It may feel like you need to be open to anything in order to find someone, but if you narrow the scope of your ask it actually makes it easier to say yes.

Figure out what you bring to the table and offer that as support to your hoped for mentor. I always like to bring someone on board who has something to offer the project. I believe in mentoring across and love the things I have learned from the folks I've mentored.

Imposter Syndrome

There is a difference between being unqualified and feeling like you might not do it perfectly. It's important to remember that it isn't our job to know all the answers. We can help find the answers. Sometimes this means hiring a consultant, working as part of an intimacy team or passing the job to someone else you know is the perfect fit.

For Producers and Directors

I know that there are a lot of demands on your time and finding a seemingly obvious mark of professionalism, such as certification or the SAG-AFTRA registry, would be an easy way to determine qualification. So, thank you for investing your time in understanding the field and seeking to learn how to better interview an IP for your project.

"SAG-AFTRA believes that intimacy coordinators should be hired in scenes involving nudity or simulated sex or upon request for other intimate and hyper-exposed scenes," so that is a good jumping off place. However, every process has different needs. If you are a director, ask yourself if staging other acts of physical intimacy is your forte or if your film would be served by having someone on set during all the moments of physical intimacy. In this case, the IC will collaborate with you and the actors around the full arc of the intimacy, taking that off your plate, so you can focus on the big picture. Depending on the amount of time an IC is needed, they can be paid a day rate or a weekly rate. Keep in mind that, for every day on set, there will also be a half to a full day of prep.

The good news is it isn't really so different from how you interview for other jobs. As you begin to understand the job and the way an intimacy professional can work, you will learn which of the IP skills and styles you find most supportive.

If an IP can describe the way they work, then you can rest assured that they have a process and are clear on how they use it. Ask about their strengths and specialties. Ask potential IPs how they handle conflict with those in power. Have they worked on similar projects and what kinds of things did they consider in their risk assessment? Ask how they work as a choreographer, what vocabulary they use. What kind of time considerations do they take into account? What are their closure practices?

Choosing Your Team

Remembering that while working with people you know can be great because you may already have a shared vocabulary, if your project includes specialties, it can also lead to settling for someone who isn't the best fit. Additionally, it can lead to unintentional gatekeeping. Broadening your circle of collaborators allows the industry to grow and diversify while helping your project have the best chance for success.

Bibliography

SAG-AFTRA. "Standards Protocols for the Use of Intimacy Coordinators." *SAG-AFTRA*, https://www.sagaftra.org/files/sa_documents/SA_IntimacyCoord.pdf.

"View Registry." *SAG-AFTRA*, https://www.sagaftra.org/contracts-industry-resources/workplace-harassment-prevention/intimacy-coordinator-resources/view.

Adapting to the Actor's Process

Laura Rikard

> Laura Rikard is a co-founder and head faculty of Theatrical Intimacy Education and a contributor to *Staging Sex*. She has received the Kennedy Center Medallion for her contributions to intimacy direction. When I was inviting folks to write for this book, I asked Laura what she was most passionate to talk about right now, and she suggested this chapter on adapting to the actor's process. I was so excited about getting a diversity of voices into this book with different skills and ideas, because no one person or pedagogy will be right for everyone. Ultimately, I hope this book offers something for everyone and that each developing artist can take what works for them and leave what they don't need at any given moment, adapting to the creative team and situation.

Understanding Process

The work of intimacy professionals is directly in conversation with – and in service to – the actor's process. My job is to facilitate that process, not to discipline it, but to use my expertise to help actors do their best work. Too often, ICs presume their own process is more important than adapting to serve the collaboration with the production team. This is problematic; it can create distrust and frustration among collaborators.

I just spoke with an actor. In discussing tomorrow's scene they commented, "I feel great about tomorrow. I've spoken with my co-star and director. It's pretty clear what's needed. This is really a courtesy call. I don't have much to discuss. I trust the director to get the scene she wants and to respect us." I am delighted that the actor's "trust" lies with the director. I am grateful the actor feels that their co-star trusts them and is confidently communicating their boundaries. And, it is perfectly acceptable that they referred to our conversation as "a courtesy call."

My process pulls from an enormous toolshed of skills for filming intimacy, but often only one small tool in that shed needs to be used. When we shoot this scene later this week, I may have little to do *in the room* because I coordinated clear communication *in advance*, making only part of my full toolkit necessary. The coordination skills I implemented prior to filming ensured I will not need to use every skill I have this week; not every job requires every available tool.

One of the most important skills employed in intimacy coordination is the IC's ability to adapt their process by reading and responding to the needs in the room. I have assessed that this current project is guided by consent-based leadership. The production team, actors and other departments have welcomed an IC in collaboration. I have witnessed boundaries being communicated and respected without justification across multiple power dynamics. I have watched actors communicate about the movements of physical intimacy and seek guidance from me when necessary. The director has been thoughtful and transparent with the actors about the choreographic expectations and given the actors space to contribute to it. When everything is working well, I need only be sensitive and step back.

The Goals of Process

When training intimacy professionals, I offer a full range of tools to empower competent ICs to enter and adjust to each production, this comes with the understanding that rarely will all tools be needed on each production. The training objective is to equip each IC's toolkit so they can select and utilize tools appropriately. We don't use a table saw to fix a broken lamp; you might not need boundary practice. Two actors may have been clearly and professionally communicating their boundaries before the IC was hired; the IC's presence shouldn't disrupt that communication. If an intimacy professional were to mandate that only an IC can establish boundaries that would ignore the skills actors may have to set their own boundaries with each other.

Forcing them to do a process with an IC they do not agree with may cross their boundaries. Actors should have the autonomy to be able to do this on any day, not just when an IC is present.

After the #MeToo movement, intimacy professionals were hired and implemented before the industry, production companies or unions had a clear understanding of what the role looks like when integrated appropriately. Influential governing bodies within the industry created protocols and guidelines about how to work with folks in this discipline. But one key community left out of the conversation while formalizing guidelines around intimacy was the actors themselves. Many actors have confided their frustrations with the lack of conversation some intimacy professionals have had with them to see how their process works in collaboration.

I have worked as an IC with many actors who, following our collaboration, will express their concerns, asking: "Why is this a much better experience than what I've had before? I didn't want to say this because I didn't want you to think I was a problem, but I have really hated working with intimacy professionals." I want to end this pattern; I want to see more intimacy professionals get work because actors have *good* experiences with them. With the best of intentions, too many intimacy professionals have shown up in spaces aiming to impose their process and point of view, causing actors and production teams to feel policed rather than supported. This has raised concerns among actors, producers, directors and crew members that ICs are working to protect others from their personal traumatic experiences rather than honestly and fairly assessing their current project's needs.

In a consent-based process, the intimacy professional shouldn't mandate a process; they should assess the actor's process, offering appropriate support when needed. This requires ICs to be curious and respectful regarding the actor's process, thoughtful about actors' experiences, and humble about where the IC's tools are needed – and not needed. One of the most beautiful things about hiring an intimacy professional is that they can be great mediators. Their job first and foremost is to make sure everyone is on the same page. If ego or inflexibility is driving their decisions, they are not going to be useful in helping balance out what is always going to be an imbalance of power. Intimacy professionals must guard against allowing themselves to get caught up in the system that their very presence is supposed to help equalize.

Intimacy as a discipline has more in common with acting than is often noted. Most comparisons are made to fight or dance choreography. It must be noted that intimacy is its own choreographic discipline with its own nuances. The movements of dance, fight and intimacy have vastly different psychological impacts upon performers. Fighting and dance choreography are not part of everyday pedestrian life, and do not necessarily exist in everyone's daily activities. Webster's dictionary defines intimacy as "the state of being intimate: FAMILIARITY." Familiarity lives in everyone's being all the time and plays out in different ways in our lives, unlike fight and dance, which is why blanketing the same principles of those choreographic disciplines may lead to confusion. All humans live within their own being of this state and practice it daily. This distinction of intimacy from fight and dance does not negate the similarities that exist, but we must also acknowledge their significant differences.

Honoring Actor Process

Theatrical intimacy in all forms doesn't begin or end on the days an intimacy professional is at rehearsal or on set. The acting process from the very beginning is a deeply intimate and personal process that every actor is navigating, exploring and reckoning with from the time they learn their first line. Whether an actor's training is from a conventional institution like a college or university training program or they have trained through professional practice, how actors practice their craft is deeply personal. The actor's voice is imperative to this conversation and the work of the intimacy professional is to come in as a collaborator, to observe and understand the unique artistic process of that particular production and integrate the tools from their skillset needed to support the production.

When working with actors, be curious about their process, be excited to have conversations about what they bring to the table, and, in turn, they will be more excited to ask questions, and to learn about the IC's tools.

Trust takes time to build. Intimacy professionals are rarely, if ever, part of the process every day. It is natural for the actors to build more trust with the members of the production team who are present daily. The limited intimate scenes in scripts limit the time an intimacy professional is going to be budgeted, and no one's going to have automatic trust in someone simply because of a title.

Some tips for an IC when first meeting actors: work from open ended questions, gather information and state back to them what is heard. Ask them about their interpretation of the scene or story. Ask what thoughts, questions and concerns they have. Talk through how the scene's going to work. Is the setting working for them? Have they thought about what modesty garments would be useful? How do they feel about you explaining barriers or modesty garments? Never promise a "safe space," because safety is subjective and cannot be guaranteed, as explained in the 2023 article I wrote with Amanda Rose Villarreal, "Focus on Impact, Not Intention: Moving from 'Safe' Spaces to Spaces of Acceptable Risk." These tips are a successful way to open the work for collaboration. Another good tip is to assume positive intent. Make no assumptions that there is anything that needs to be "fixed." Work from process and do the actions of the job.

When the actor said to me, "I trust the director," I thought, "Yeah, that's as it should be." Some ICs' egos would've been bruised when actors didn't say, "I trust you to take care of this scene." But this collaboration isn't about me, and I understand that the actor doesn't know me. Furthermore, actors will not trust an IC who seems to be pushing their presence or agenda on the actor's process. They will be more excited to collaborate with an IC who shows curiosity and care regarding their process.

Bibliography

Rikard, Laura and Amanda Rose Villarreal. (2023) "Focus on Impact, Not Intention: Moving from 'Safe' Spaces to Spaces of Acceptable Risk." *Journal of Consent-Based Performance*, vol. 2, no. 1, 1, February, pp. 1–16. https://doi.org/10.46787/jcbp.v2i1.3646.

Hopes for the Industry   21

Moderated by
Brooke M. Haney

There were so many incredible intimacy professionals that contributed to this book. For our final chapter, I wanted to give a sense of what challenges we face right now and where we see the future of this industry.

BROOKE	When I think about my identity as a white, queer, gender-queer person, I know my practice is impacted by the privilege I've had as a white, cis-passing/most often femme-presenting, straight sized person. While I deserve credit for my expertise and the contributions I've made to the field, that part of my identity has opened doors for me through both unconscious and conscious bias. As far as my queerness goes, perhaps the biggest influence on my work is that my definition of sex is expansive and I have a strong desire to show that in my choreography. How does your identity impact your practice?
CESSALEE STOVALL	I'm typically hired when identity is a visible marker of diversity, which is great. I love supporting works for folks who have historically been disempowered in the craft.

AMANDA CUTTING	As a fat woman, I bring a lot of awareness to how actors perceive their bodies and the importance of diverse representation of bodies on screen.
KIM SHIVELY	I don't think anyone needs to be a parent in order to work with minors, but having children who are vastly different from one another and coming from a family full of neurodiversity greatly impacts my practice. I approach each person remembering that they are someone's family member, someone's child. It keeps me in the process as I tend to focus easily on product.
KAJA DUNN	The erasure of people of color and racialized tropes that so often show up in the world of theatre and film (including in my own career) were the impetus for me to dive deeper and interrogate the work of intimacy. In addition, I have a background in women and gender studies and Africana studies, as well as a knowledge of what it's like to have somebody impose things on your body when they don't understand you or your culture. All this deepened my commitment to make sure that I had strong cultural competency stemming from Black feminism and the feminist theories of other people of color in my own work.
LEO MOCK	My non-binary identity contributes to a non-binary practice. I feel comfortable working with multiplicities of truth and experience, I am open to non-linear creative practices, and I believe in striving for fulfillment over perfectionism. Non-binary consent means, for me, that we are risk-aware, making decisions that work for now, and making room for fluidity.
ROBBIE TAYLOR HUNT	Being a male intimacy coordinator becomes a factor in my work a lot. Of course, I am considerate of the fact that TV and film sets are dominated by men, particularly in HOD roles and the crew likely to remain in a closed set, and I don't want to be another male presence if it makes an actor uncomfortable. However, I am also wary that my job includes being aware of power dynamics in a

space and mitigating against them, and I'm trained to protect actors against power imbalances no matter what they're stemming from (gender, age, sexuality, etc.).

The calling into question that my appropriateness for the work because of my gender raises many identity-based questions for me. Are they assuming I'm straight and therefore might be attracted to a female actor? Should I tell them I'm queer? Are they assuming my female IC peers are straight? What about my non-binary and/or Trans IC colleagues? Is it about wanting to see someone in the space that "looks female?" Or is it about relating to the experience of being a woman in a male-dominated space, so then perhaps some of my Trans/NB IC peers share that experience?

I've had an actor explicitly ask me if I'm gay, which I'm happy to disclose, but it feels strange having to flog my queer credentials in the workplace.

ELI LYNN
I am Trans and non-binary, as well as neurodivergent, and while I think all of these things impact my practice in very important ways, it can be difficult to isolate their effects because they are intrinsic to and inseparable from everything else about me. I think the biggest thing is that being queer and Trans has allowed me to be an important advocate for queer/Trans actors in rooms where very often they have no other advocates. My neurodivergent identity doesn't come up as often in the room, but I think it does allow me to adapt to actor needs in a way that perhaps I would be less adept at if I wasn't already familiar with navigating certain needs for myself.

BROOKE
Does your identity affect the jobs you will take?

ELI
There have been a couple of situations where I knew a company or institution had a reputation for being an uphill battle for LGBTQ+ people, and while that alone isn't grounds in my mind for rejecting a job, it's definitely factored into my

	decision. If I'm not being compensated enough to balance out the emotional labor it's going to take to constantly be advocating for MYSELF in a space, then I'd rather not. The flip side of that coin is that if I know there are LGBTQ+ actors, or it is a queer story that is being told, I'm more likely to try and take the job so I can help make the space safer.
BROOKE	I have worked on many queer projects helmed or crewed by straight folks. When I have the opportunity to work on a queer project with queer collaborators, that is my church! It's only happened a handful of times so far, and I love all my work, but those are the jobs I live for.
LEO	For the first time, I recently experienced a director's hesitation to hire me because I use "he/him" pronouns. I am reluctant to take work with anyone who sees my Transness (or masculinity) as a threat to their safety or the safety of their collaborators, because that work will likely get in the way of the actual job. In works that feature identities and cultures that are not part of my lived experience, I prefer to assist intimacy professionals who do have those lived experiences (if I work on the project at all).
ROBBIE	Considering whether I'm the right person for a job, I think about my lived experience, professional training and experience, learned experience, and the needs of the performers and production. My feeling is that we need to have a complex, nuanced sense of how our identity plays into the jobs we take.
KAJA	Often it means I'm only called in if someone is specifically seeking a Black woman or a POC. I center and seek out work with my own community, Black people, and I'm very proud of the work I've done specifically with Black women and the Black queer community.
	But I also have substantial skills and knowledge around other marginalized groups and

global majority groups. What can be frustrating is that whiteness is so often equated with superior competence and white intimacy professionals are given work from all of our cultures. The rest of us often are only given work from our specific culture, and often only when someone pushes to hire us, or it's a gig others don't want or can't do.

CESSALEE: I sometimes give discounts to work that is full of artists of colour.

AMANDA M. EDWARDS: I am happy to make recommendations for other qualified professionals when I determine a project is outside of my scope of practice for any reason, especially if my presence (as a white, cis, Ashkenazi Jewish looking woman) could potentially cause harm.

BROOKE: What is one of the biggest challenges of our job?

AMANDA C: The expectation that this is a solo job. Meaning a department of one. That's not sustainable. To make a living, IPs have to take on multiple shows, increasing the probability of burnout. Working with a team of people allows for breaks, sharing the workload and financial sustainability.

KAJA: Racism and a lack of clear standards for our contracts. Many white practitioners are profiting off of the knowledge and creative work of POCs, but state publicly that there is a lack or we don't exist.

KIM: Time. Time and lack of information. There are a lot of people doing the best they can with the information they have, but unfortunately the information is not serving them or the people they are working with. It's a real challenge to get people the right IC for the right job under the pressure of time and money.

CESSALEE: Gatekeeping.

LAURA RIKARD: The industry does not understand how to assess if an IC is qualified. There are too many people getting work who do not understand the process and this is due to the fact that the industry jumped into hiring this role before they understood what its process is or how to hire. The biggest challenge is

	that the folks who have gotten the most publicity around this work are trying to create a monopoly, overcharge "certifications," have influence over influential decision makers in the industry, and work from a patriarchal point of view, and this contradicts the very things this work is supposed to do, which is to dismantle power dynamics.
ROBBIE	There are some key principles to this work. Beyond that, there is – and should be – a diversity of approaches to intimacy coordination, including pedagogies, concepts, ideologies, artistic backgrounds, professional backgrounds, etc.
ELI	I think a lot of large and powerful institutions remain unconvinced of the need for qualified intimacy professionals, which results in either nobody being hired at all, or hiring someone who isn't qualified just so they can underpay them and check the box. It's particularly depressing when a company with a lot of resources refuses to budget appropriately for ID work – especially when I know so many small companies who are working as hard as they can to compensate people fairly.
AMANDA E.	It seems as though the scarcity mindset, pervasive in the entertainment industry, permeates the intimacy profession as well, which has led to gatekeeping and exclusion.
LEO	Economic and resource barriers mean that the field is fairly homogenous right now, and the most powerful and privileged people are dictating what qualifies an intimacy professional to work.
BROOKE	We are so often in the place of making space for others and their boundaries. We can have boundaries too. What boundaries do you set for yourself around the job?
CESSALEE	I don't need to say yes, if I feel like it will be an emotional drain on me, or if I don't feel empowered in the team (by having too little time, too great of expectations). If someone says I have two hours, I say then I can do a workshop, no more.
ELI	The biggest one is the energetic and emotional boundary of my own work/life balance. Before

	the pandemic, I would often be working on between five and eight projects simultaneously. While I still find myself stacking multiple projects, I am learning to be able to say "no" to things that are going to lead to overwhelm. Because not only will I be unhappy in that situation, I also won't be able to show up and do my best work.
KIM	I have boundaries around time and how much I am away from my young family. I do have a strong ethical drive, so I don't work on stories that contain violence toward children, or violence and intimacy that do not move the story forward.
LEO	I refuse to be a mental healthcare provider, and I do not make space for trauma disclosures in the rehearsal room (or with me outside of the rehearsal room). In the room where I am one of two or few Trans people, I take a lot of care around emotional bonding over that connection, and make sure it doesn't get in the way of supporting others in the process, or that we become dependent upon each other for emotional/mental support.
BROOKE	I do my best to keep a boundary where I will not work on projects where non-consent is disguised as romance. What do you think the best version of our work looks like?
ROBBIE	When everyone on a production is on board with the importance of, and ethos behind, intimacy coordination, we are able to do our best work. Until then, we are (at best) distracted or (at worst) firefighting. If the work is fully embraced, it is productive, it is efficient, it is dynamic, it is collaborative, it is a craft, it is reassuring, it is freeing.
CESSALEE	Present, uplifting each other, more collective work to build best practices and lessen competition, not being undermined in the media by celebrities.
KIM	An actor wants an IC, asks for one, and gets a great IC who makes the set and everyone there have a good day at work. Or a famous actor with a ton of power is working with another established actor with a lot of power and they don't want an

LEO	IC, so they don't have to have one. An IC can consult with wardrobe and production to make sure the actors have options, but an IC isn't stuck on set hiding from an award-winning actor when they could be out hiking or making cookies with their kids, or taking another job where they are needed. I think our best work can be telling stories to an audience that are ambiguous, messy, weird and unclear. I think our best work can be for us, as in, this is for the people in the audience who know this experience. I think our best work is done slowly. I think our best work is also done with a tiny budget and no time, and with people who are ready to get campy. I think our best work can leave audiences with more questions than answers.
BROOKE	Currently, it's 2023. What do you hope the industry looks like in 10 years? For me, one of the things I hope for is that the consent part of our work is so ingrained in the industry, that we are primarily called upon as choreographers and that the intimacy community thrives in our diversity of voices, lenses, opinions and specialties.
AMANDA E.	Inclusive and filled with integrity.
LEO	Black and brown and Indigenous and Trans and disabled.
KIM	I hope a lot of us work ourselves out of our jobs and make way for more diversity and representation in the industry. I hope that people are as concerned with sustainable work environments as they are with bottom lines. I hope producers put the well-being of every person on a production ahead of anything else. I also hope we tell good stories.
ROBBIE	As nice as it is when people are amazed that I'm there and grateful, I hope in 10 years that has faded away, and it'll be so standard that people are appreciative but don't expect anything less. I hope there is an appreciation of people's diverse backgrounds into intimacy practice, and then a cross-pollination of ideas, techniques and

experiences. Having colleagues from differing pedagogies or with unique skill sets benefits the whole community if we build and maintain a robust space for sharing.

BROOKE So, what advice do you have for the next generation of intimacy professionals?

CHA Don't forget to play, create, generate, expand. This work is so often linked to trauma and fear and saying "no!" that it can sometimes turn in on itself and become distorted until it doesn't allow room for healing and joy and "yes!" The true work honors both our limitations and our infiniteness.

LEO Don't be afraid to try weird stuff. Trust your collaborators. Spend a lot of time on foundational stuff in rehearsal so you can take big swings in choreography. Collaborate with each other. Share more information with one another. Have a post-work ritual. Have fulfilling hobbies outside of the work.

AMANDA C. Pace yourself and set clear boundaries of what projects you're willing to work on before you start the work. You don't have to be everywhere at once. Build your community and team to work together, not against each other, so you have support and colleagues to contact for the opportunity to work together.

KIM Don't try to make a full time living with IC work. Find a way to be housed in production and work in a variety of positions that support healthy workplaces. An IC is not needed for every job and having people in development helping assess what projects need what support so that budgets are built in a sustainable way would make everyone's life easier.

ELI Keep your standards high, but never gatekeep.

KAJA Find people who will be in your corner and cheer you on. Develop a strong community and give back to it as well as being nurtured by it. Take the time to learn how to do the dramaturgical work that goes with our job. It's not just fight choreography for sex.

ROBBIE	Be patient. As I was working in what I consider some of the "formative years" in the UK (although not the VERY formative years of my predecessors!) I jumped onto some bigger jobs fairly early that felt like a real stretch. I handled them well enough, but if things had gone badly it could have seriously knocked my confidence or hurt my reputation. That's never worth it, even if an opportunity seems exciting. Start on less intense jobs, build your craft, get used to the language coming out of your mouth, it takes time. There is always going to be work, and there will always be more projects and other opportunities.

Also, find solace and refuge in your IC peers. They're the only people who will ever really understand what it's like! So build those connections and maintain them.

CESSALEE	Believe in yourself, learn as much as you can about conflict management, mental health, artist well-being. It's not all about what boxes you have left to check off, it's about what work makes you YOU.

Index

ableism 20, 24, 26
actor intake meeting 78, 134, 145
aftercare 134, 136
allergies 110, 135–6, 181
anal 102, 108, 111–13, 115
anus 112–15, 153

barrier garment 6, 12, 78, 105, 114, 183, 201
BDSM 4, 8, 18–20, 23, 37, 122–9, 150
The Best Man 95–8
big big love 79
Billions 123
binding 103–4, 116
Birder 138, 149
Blank, Hanne 79
Broadcasting, Entertainment, Communications, and Theatre Union (BECTU) 101
Bonding 122, 124
budget 6, 11, 138, 150, 166–7, 194, 210–11
Burke, Tarana 86
bystander intervention 10–11

certification 9, 34, 40, 192–3, 196, 208
closed set 81, 124, 145, 176, 204
closure 8, 13, 45–6, 51, 136, 141, 146–7, 161, 171, 196
colonialism 91
contracts 26, 168
cultural competency 5, 9, 20–4, 32, 35, 76, 86, 204

The Deuce 165
Disclosure 116
doula 5–6

East New York 164, 176
Empire 59, 79

The Fat Lip Podcast 75
fatphobia 74–5, 77–8, 147
fawn response 10, 54, 144, 146
fetishization 42, 63, 64, 76
Fielding, Lucie 116

gender consultants 101, 103
global majority intimacy conference 129

Harlem 57, 59–60
Head over Heels 79
hooks, bell 86

I May Destroy You 110
intersectionality 26, 58, 156
the intimacy captain 187–91
intimacy coordinators of color 189
Intimacy Directors International 146, 179
intimask 114–15

kink 4, 8, 18, 20, 23, 37–8, 63–4, 77, 108, 111, 123–4, 126, 128–34, 150
The Kink Academy 126

Landau, Emily 67
The Last of Us 113
lesbian 15, 38, 77, 106–10, 116
Lesbian Herstory Archives 116
Love on the Run 81–2
lubrication 79, 112, 185
The L Word: Generation Q 66

Magic Mike XXL 79
masking 12, 104, 162, 185
mentorship 195
merkins 183
#MeToo Movement 158, 175, 200
minors 33, 52–6, 204
modesty garments 12, 78, 83, 103–5, 114, 138, 183–4, 201
Morrison, Toni 86

The National Society of Intimacy Professional 179
New Lives 143
non-apparent disability 9, 62–3
Novelli, Alison 80–2
nudity 21, 96, 105, 122, 124, 143, 145, 195–6
nudity rider 122, 124
NYPD Blue 174–5

O'Brien, Ita 17
Ockler, Judi Lewis 146

packers 104–5, 184
Peterson, Britta Joy 170
Polite Society 131
power dynamics 10–11, 23, 32, 108, 123, 125, 169, 171–2, 199, 204, 208
Principal Intimacy Professionals 179
prosthetics 12, 104, 105, 138, 179–85

qualification 34, 44, 187, 192–7
queer intimacy 100–17, 184

rigger 1, 129, 132–3, 135–6
risk assessment 10, 11, 194, 196

Rodis, Alicia 118–19, 165
Resentment 84

scope of practice 1–7, 14, 19, 31, 34, 52, 55, 142–3, 147, 155, 162, 171, 207
self-care 13, 39, 116, 121, 142, 146–7, 162
sexual violence 27, 155–63
She Kills Monsters 147
She's Clean 143
Shibari 133, 135
Shibari Study 137
Shrill 79
simulated sex 12, 21, 74, 78–82, 95–6, 106, 110, 114, 122, 143, 194, 196
Sins Invalid: An Unshamed Claim to Beauty 67
Skin, Tooth, and Bone: The Basis of Movement is Our People 67
Special 66
special effects 125, 179, 180
Stage A Change 40
Staging Sex: Best Practices, Tools, and Techniques 67, 109, 146, 198
Stranger by the Lake 113

Tales of the City 112
Theatrical Intimacy Education 85, 101, 191, 198
Thunder Force 97
Transtape 116
trauma informed practices 11, 26, 33, 145
trauma response 54, 159
tropes 9, 63, 64, 76, 85–6, 88–92
tucking 103, 104, 185

unclockable 116

Venus 76

wardrobe 12, 78, 82, 103, 104, 110, 123, 124, 125, 160, 171, 210
The Weekend 113

For Product Safety Concerns and Information please contact our EU representative GPSR@taylorandfrancis.com
Taylor & Francis Verlag GmbH, Kaufingerstraße 24, 80331 München, Germany

www.ingramcontent.com/pod-product-compliance
Lightning Source LLC
Chambersburg PA
CBHW052107300426
44116CB00010B/1565